Umbrella Co

Umbrella Cockatoos Book for Keeping, Pros and Cons, Care, Housing, Diet and Health.
by

Roger Rodendale

Table of Contents

Introduction

If a big, cuddly and rather noisy pet is what you are looking for, then the Umbrella Cockatoo is perfect for you. The largest among the different species of cockatoos, this magnificent bird has beautiful white plumes that are complete with crown feathers that fan out to look like an umbrella, and hence the name.

These birds make wonderful pets as they are extremely intelligent and affectionate towards their humans. However, providing your Umbrella cockatoo with the right care and affection is a must if you want to give him a long and healthy life.

You see, like all parrots, these birds too require a lot of mental stimulation and exercise. The biggest issue that most owners face with these birds is the noise that they make. Whether they are happy, sad, excited or angry, Umbrella Cockatoos tend to be very vocal and quite loud. This is one of the many reasons why these birds end up in shelters and rescue homes.

If you are planning to bring home an Umbrella Cockatoo, it is very important that you learn about the different behavioral aspects of this bird and the right care requirements. Although these birds are gentle giants, the sheer size and power of their jaws and their claws make them a hazard if they develop issues like aggression or even fear.

Once you learn how to care for them, these birds are extremely fun to have around. They are playful birds that will keep you entertained all day long. You will have a great time watching the bird climb around the cage and perform goofy tricks for you. Of course, these birds can learn to talk as well. They are gentle giants that will allow you to cuddle and pet them once they are hand tamed.

This book will tell you everything that you need to know about an Umbrella Cockatoo right from the time you bring your bird home. You will learn about the most popular sources to get your bird home from. The book covers simple tricks that will help you train your bird to be more social and relaxed in his new home. Most importantly, the book covers the various healthcare issues that your bird may face to help you provide the best possible care.

In this book, you will find information sourced from individuals who have owned an Umbrella cockatoo before for the most practical solutions to any roadblocks that you may hit on the way. The more you learn about your bird, the better. This book is certainly a great way to begin your journey with your bird and understand his exact needs and requirements.

Chapter 1: About the Umbrella Cockatoo

Also known as the White Crested Cockatoo or the White Cockatoo, the Umbrella Cockatoo is the first image that pops in your mind when you think of this bird. These birds are among the largest and most popular species of cockatoos found in the world. Their compatibility with humans makes them extremely popular pets. They are fun to be around and make a wonderful addition to your family for several reasons.

This chapter tells you all about the natural history of these birds and their natural behavior to help you understand what they will need when you raise them in your home.

1. Physical Traits

These are medium to large sized birds with a characteristic fan shaped crest feathers. These feathers have blunt ends and are broad. Like most cockatoos, these birds also have yellow underwings and also under tails.

The crest feathers are rather complex and can be opened to look like a fan. These feathers are normally unfolded when the bird is upset, surprised or is trying to show dominance. Because of the umbrella-like appearance of these crest feathers, these birds get their name.

Cockatoos are also known for a wide variety of colors that are seen on the plumes. However, these birds are white in color for the most part. The solid white plumes earn them the name "White Cockatoo". The only coloration that is seen is the yellow feathers under the tail and the wings. These yellow feathers are most visible when the bird takes flight or when he opens his wings.

An adult umbrella cockatoo can grow up to 18 inches in length and will weigh about 400g in the case of females and 800g in the case of males. The male and the female are almost identical to look at, barring some minor differences. For instance, in the case of the male Umbrella Cockatoos, the beak is slightly bigger in size. Usually the male and the female have dark black or brown eyes. The color of the iris varies depending upon the gender, however. In the case of mature females, the color of the iris may be brownish or reddish while males have darker irises that are black or brown in color. The head is also slightly smaller in the case of the female.

When the crest of this bird is resting, the shape of the head is quite similar to the Salmon Crested Cockatoo. However, the White Cockatoo is much sleeker in shape and the shape and color of the crest are quite different. In the case of the Salmon Crested Cockatoo, the plumes have a pinkish infusion.

These birds have short feathers that tend to cover the upper legs closely. They also tend to drop some feather dust that is very similar to talcum powder and can be easily transferred to your clothes.

One factor that cockatoos have in common with other parrot species is the zygodactyl feet. This means that their feet have four toes in total, with two facing the front and two facing the back. This allows them to be great climbers, helps them perch easily, grab different objects and also use their toes to break or hold food.

The beak has a characteristic hook shape with the upper mandible bending over the lower one. The beak and the feet are usually dark grey in color, contrasting the rest of the body.

2. Habitat and distribution

The natural range and habitat of cockatoos differ from one species to another. No two species of these birds are alike when it comes to their natural behavior, range and habitat, with the influence being primarily from the country of origin. For instance, cockatoo species that originate in Australia normally live in huge flocks and are mostly found in open spaces. There are other species that do not gather in flocks that are as big and tend to hide in tree canopies for the most part of the day.

Umbrella Cockatoos are tropical birds that usually live in sub-tropical and tropical forests and are mostly seen at the edge of a forest.

One common thing between all species of cockatoos is that they normally make their nest in the hollows of trees. The holes are not made by the birds themselves. They look for hollow spaces in tree trunks that can be easily accessed. When they find a suitable nesting space, these birds may alter the size of the entrance and the exit as needed. These nests cover a large area depending upon the size of the flock.

Umbrella Cockatoos are normally seen in wooded areas. This includes large woodland areas, swamps, mangroves and agricultural areas as well. These birds can also be seen around the edges of rivers and forest clearings. They are normally found in tree canopies. This mostly includes tall trees that are part of the secondary vegetation. These birds are seen at elevations of 300 to 900 meters.

These birds are native to Indonesia, with a major population living in the North Molucacas in the Maluku province. They are also seen on the islands of Bacan, Halmahera, Ternate, Kasiruta, Mandioli and Tidore. Some cockatoos have also been found on the Obi island along with the satellite island Bisa. It is believed that these populations were introduced by several Umbrella Cockatoos escaping captivity.

Today, these birds are bred in captivity across the globe and are among the most popular species of cockatoos.

3. Captive History

It was around the 1850s that cockatoos were first discovered by sailors from Europe. These sailors interacted with these birds when they traveled to Eastern countries, Indonesia in particular. Several dead specimens of these birds were brought back by sailors to show collectors and scientists of their new discovery.

Following this, some live birds were also taken back to Europe as trophies of their travel. In the native countries, these birds were already popularly kept as pets. They had been domesticated for several decades.

It was in the year 1900 that European aristocrats began to show interest in these birds along with other exotic parrot species. At that time, these birds were imported directly from their natural habitats. It was not until 1985 that these birds were bred in captivity. The first ever captive breeding of this bird was successfully completed in the Netherlands. Today, most birds that are found as pets are bred in captivity.

These birds are protected by strict laws because of their highly threatened natural population. These laws have also been put in place to prevent any influx of diseases when importing these birds.

Today, Umbrella Cockatoos continue to rise in numbers in the UK, USA and Europe. One trend that has been observed with these birds is that people prefer to purchase baby cockatoos that are easier to train and handle. As a result, several adult cockatoos have been abandoned. Therefore, it is important to understand how to handle these birds carefully to prevent any unwarranted bites and issues.

The first ever description of the Umbrella Cockatoo was made by Philips Ludwig Satius Miller. At this time, the birds were named "cacatula alba" derived from the Latin word Alba which means white.

For a long time, these birds were referred to as white parrots. Although this continues today, it is quite inaccurate as White Cockatoos are not true parrots although they belong to a parrot family called Cocatuidae.

4. Different senses in Umbrella Cockatoos

Cockatoos have the same senses as human beings. However, the manner in which they use the sense of hearing, touch, sight, smell and taste can be quite different. These senses play a very important role in understanding the needs and the behavior of these birds. This section explores the various sensory adaptations of this bird:

Umbrella cockatoo hearing

Most people wonder if birds have any ears at all. And, if they do, where are these ears placed? The positioning of the ears in cockatoos is quite similar to the way they are positioned in human beings. The only difference is that with birds, the ear is simply a hole that is covered by their plumes. They do not have any external ears, like other animals.

With cockatoos, this is one of the most sensitive organs. In the wild, these birds use their excellent ability to hear as a way of staying in contact with other birds from their flock. They also use their hearing abilities to know if any predator is lurking around. This is why cockatoos tend to scream incessantly in order to stay in touch with each other. This is a habit that you may find with the bird you bring home, too.

Umbrella Cockatoo vision

Umbrella Cockatoos are able to see color. In fact, their color vision is much better in comparison to human beings. This is primarily because the four pigments in their retina are light-sensitive. In comparison to this, humans have three different pigments. These pigments are activated by lights of various wavelengths. This sends signals to the brain that is able to perceive the color. In the case of cockatoos, this fourth pigment is also sensitive to ultraviolet rays. This light is invisible for human beings but adds another wavelength to the colors that cockatoos are able to perceive.

There is another interesting aspect that differentiates the vision of these birds and human beings. Cockatoos are able to perceive more images each second in comparison to humans. This is why they are able to see any fast movement more clearly than us. This ability comes extremely handy when the birds are in flight.

Night vision in humans and cockatoos are just about the same, each being unable to see too well in the dark.

For cockatoos, sight is extremely important to help them find food and shelter. It also helps them locate other members of their flock. In other animals such as rodents and dogs, this depends entirely on touch and smell. Hearing is the second most important sense in these birds.

The eyes of these birds are placed on either side of the head. This allows them to see around them, almost to 360 degrees. They do not have great perception of depth because the field of vision does not overlap very well. These birds actually tilt their head when they have to look up, just as we tilt our head back to do so.

Umbrella Cockatoo touch
Unlike what you would expect, the umbrella cockatoo does not use its feet to touch. Instead, the beak and the tongue are used to feel the texture of any object. They usually bite the object to see if it is hard or soft. This is one of the primary reasons why these birds will take a nip at your finger during step up training.

Umbrella Cockatoo taste
These birds use the tongue to taste just like human beings. Their tongue functions quite differently, however. They have a dry and dark colored tip to their tongue. This part of their tongue is unable to perceive any taste. It is used only to feel the texture of the food and to peel the food or push it to the back of their tongue.

The back of their tongue is pink in color and is moist, allowing them to taste what they eat. If the bird wants to really taste what he is eating, he will first touch the food using the tip and then take it to the back of his bill. This allows the food to stick to the tasting part.

Umbrella Cockatoo smell
These birds do not have the best sense of smell. For the most part, they rely on their hearing abilities and sight to find their way around in the wild. The part of the brain that processes different smells is very small in birds like cockatoos and other species of parrots. This indicates that they do not have a very well developed sense of smell.

The way these birds perceive the world around them is responsible for a large part of their behavior. This is why it is important for a cockatoo owner to understand these different senses. Be it screaming, the way they interact with food or even the kind of toys that they pick, their different senses have a large role to play in it.

5. Natural behavior of Umbrella Cockatoos

Umbrella cockatoos are usually found in small groups, in pairs and can even be seen alone in the wild at times. When they do reside in flocks, the size of the flock is between 15 and 50 birds. These birds are usually quite social. However, birds that have formed pair bonds do not bond easily with other birds. This does not define any dominance order with these birds.

They are mostly diurnal and are also sedentary for the most part. They only move around when they are in search of food and could be nomadic when there is any scarcity of food.

These birds are extremely inquisitive and bright by nature. They are among the most advanced birds in terms of their cognitive abilities. In fact, they are able to use tools as well. For instance, these birds are often seen using sticks and twigs to scratch their body, especially the back.

This is one important trait of the cockatoo that you need to know as a pet owner. When they do not receive enough mental stimulation in captivity, these birds become very neurotic. This leads to issues like feather plucking and most of them will pluck themselves till they are almost bald when they are not adequately mentally stimulated.

As pets, these birds are extremely loving and affectionate. They love spending time with their human families and will behave almost like dogs and cats when kept as pets.

These birds rely on several noises and gestures to communicate with their flock mates. They use instruments to communicate as well, indicating their superior cognition. These birds use small wooden pieces to bang on the barks of trees or hollow logs to communicate with flock members and to also inform other birds around that the territory belongs to them.

They normally feed on fruits that are on trees. This includes durian, papaya, rambutan and langsat. There have been some instances of these birds also eating smaller insects like crickets. One habit of these birds that makes them a negative factor for human settlements is that they also feed on crops like maize. This is one of the reasons why these birds are considered to be pests in several parts of their native range. They tend to cause a lot of damage to these crops.

On the other hand, they are considered a positive factor because they eat fruits and disperse the seeds. These birds are also helpful to other species of birds in the case of nesting. Their nests in tree hollows are normally used by other birds after the breeding season is completed.

6. Mating behavior of Umbrella Cockatoos

Umbrella Cockatoos have the most elaborate and impressive courtship behavior. It starts with all the feathers of the male ruffled up to show off his body. He will spread all the feathers of the tail, extend the wings and keep his crest erect. With this impressive display, he hops around till he catches the attention of the female.

Usually the female birds avoid the male when the courting ritual begins. She warms up to him after some time. If they are compatible, they will begin to scratch one another around the tail and the head. This is known to improve bonding between two potential mates.

After this courtship display, the male will mount the female and the cloaca is joined for mating. In the case of adult birds that have already had a successful mating season, the courtship ritual is much shorter and it is the female that will approach the male first.

The bond formed between pairs is very strong and these birds remain monogamous. Once they have found a mate, this bond will last their whole life. In fact, if one of the bonded birds dies, the other one will go into extreme depression. When they are raised in captivity, these birds may also consider their owners their mate, often becoming very possessive of them.

The weather plays a very important role in the mating season of these birds. When the fauna around them is at its best, they begin to breed. Birds that have formed pair bonds will leave their flocks. Then, they look for a good nesting spot in the hollows of trees. These nesting holes are often made in the largest trees available. The trees must be at least 5-30 meters in height.

Every clutch of these birds will contain two eggs. In some cases, there may be three as well. The responsibility of incubating these eggs is shared by the pair. This takes roughly 30 days.

One very interesting trait of cockatoos is that every pair will only raise one chick from the clutch. This is usually the one that hatches first, provided that the chick is healthy and well-formed. In case of any deformity in the first hatchling, they will move on to the second one and care only for that hatchling.

After they are born, the chicks are extremely dependent on their parents for at least three weeks of their life. They will be able to fly only when they are about three months old. These birds take some time to become sexually mature, usually when they are about 6 years old.

Once the chick becomes capable of taking care of himself, the three birds will leave the nesting area and go back to their flock.

7. Conservation status of Umbrella Cockatoos

Umbrella Cockatoos have been listed among the eight threatened species that are restricted to the Northern Maluku Endemic Bird Area. One of the biggest threats to the populations of these birds is their popularity in the pet trade market. They are captured from the wild and sold as pets.

In just three years, between 1990 and 1993, 17% of the wild population of these birds was removed due to pet trade. The largest consumer of these wild Umbrella Cockatoos is the United States. An estimated 10,143 birds were imported to the US between 1990 and 1999.

However, these birds are extremely adaptable. They also have great reproducing abilities and are able to adjust to changes in their habitat. They also do not have as many predators in the wild as other species of birds. This is one of the reasons why these birds are more resistant to this immense pressure that the pet trade market puts on their wild populations. These birds are also collectively a very competitive species.

The second biggest threat to these birds is deforestation. They are also vulnerable because of hunting practices in their native areas.

Today, the Umbrella Cockatoo has been listed as a vulnerable species by the IUCN. They have been placed in the CITES Appendix II since the year 1980. Once the Indonesian government became a part of CITES in the year 1999, several quotas on hunting and trapping of these birds were issued. Unfortunately, none of these quotas were properly enforced.

From the year 1999, capturing wild specimens of these birds was made illegal altogether. Today a zero quota policy is applicable to these birds unless there is more reliable system to enforce them.

Chapter 2: The Umbrella Cockatoo as a Pet

Umbrella Cockatoos are among the most popular cockatoo species kept as pets world over. These beautiful and intelligent creatures have been domesticated and raised in captivity for several decades now. Known for forming extremely strong bonds with their owners, these birds are prized possessions of several families across the globe.

This chapter will tell you all that you need to know about having this bird at home as a pet.

1. What makes them popular?

There is no doubt that one of the primary reasons for the popularity of these birds is their beauty. These birds have gorgeous white plumes and the peculiar crest that makes it a sight for sore eyes.

Today, most cockatoo species are endangered, including this species to a certain extent. However, it is legal to have an Umbrella Cockatoo as a pet. It is important to note that any capture of these birds from the wild is illegal and is a crime often committed in the black market. When you are buying an Umbrella Cockatoo, you need to make sure that the bird has been bred in captivity.

Besides their exquisite beauty, these birds are also known to be great pets because of their personality. Of course, these birds can be quite a handful from time to time. They are known for having temper tantrums and can also become aggressive or nippy when not adequately stimulated mentally.

However, they are very cheerful birds when cared for properly. They are also extremely entertaining, providing you with hours of playful display and goofy antics to watch.

Overall, these birds make great pets as they are social and affectionate. They are known for forming special bonds with the owners and their family. They are closest to the person who provides most care for them and just love to play with this person and even give him or her cuddles and oodles of affection. This display of affection by snuggling close to the owner is very rarely seen among birds. You may not see this behavior even in other species that are very closely related to these birds.

Like most parrot species, these birds will learn to speak by mimicking different sounds. In fact, several cockatoo owners are able to teach their pets a series of words and can even help the bird learn these words in context. Of course, these birds cannot learn as many words as other species of parrots but can be quite fun to teach words to.

Umbrella Cockatoos are extremely talkative and loud birds. They have a call that is very loud and will require some getting used to. If they are alarmed or annoyed, these birds may also hiss.

Although these birds are extremely adorable and sweet when they are young, they can become extremely demanding and difficult if not trained well. You need to make sure that you are able to spend enough time with these birds to give them the care and the kind of training that they need. If you are unable to do so yourself, you can also seek help from professionals. Umbrella Cockatoos do not appreciate being ignored for too long. So make sure that you have enough time and resources when you bring one of these birds home as a pet.

2. The flipside of Umbrella Cockatoos

There is no doubt that these birds make wonderful pets. However, it is necessary for potential Umbrella Cockatoo owners to know all the cons of having this bird at home as a pet.

One of the primary reasons of several adult cockatoos being abandoned in shelters each year is the fact that people do not realize what they are signing up for. There are some important things that you must know about the flipside of owning these birds to understand how to prevent this and how to handle it as well:

- **They are extremely noisy:** The screech of an Umbrella Cockatoo can travel for 3 miles. So you can only imagine how noisy these birds can get. Instinctively, these birds cry out to their flock members at dawn and dusk, which is when you can expect maximum noise from your bird. Make sure that you have no issues with this and neither do you neighbors.

- **They can be messy:** You will find food stuff and pellets stuffed in different nooks and crannies in your house. They also tend to fling food from time to time. The floor in and around the cages will have debris from food and toys, feathers and even feather dust.

- **You will have to rework your routine:** Getting a cockatoo requires a good amount of dedication. You must ensure that the food routine is in place, the bird has ample training and play time as well. Your travel schedules will also depend upon the bird and ensure that you have someone to take care of your bird when you are away.

- **They have a very specific diet:** Giving your bird just pellets is not good enough. You will have to do some cooking for your bird too and make sure that he has a good amount of fresh produce available in his diet. Nutrition is one of the most important factors, as deficiency is the cause for several health issues with birds.

- **You have to invest in toys:** As mentioned before, these birds have very powerful cognitive skills. If you fail to stimulate your bird mentally, you make way for several behavioral issues. If your cockatoo is bored, he will develop issues like screaming, biting and even feather plucking.

- **They are expensive pets:** The initial costs of owning these birds is quite high given the housing requirements and the cost of the bird itself. Following that you need to take care of vet fees, food expenses, toys, accessories and other requirements that can eat into your budget.

- **Their size makes them quite dangerous:** The sheer size of the Umbrella Cockatoo makes them a danger to other pets or even children. Even a gentle nip can be painful and cause serious injuries because their jaws are extremely powerful. This is why most people prefer to adopt baby Umbrella Cockatoos and then raise them to be more balanced and well-behaved.

- **It is a commitment of a lifetime:** Umbrella Cockatoos are known to live up to 40 years in captivity. There are even claims of these birds living for up to 100 years, although there is no evidence to support this. So you must be prepared to devote a lifetime and even prepare the next generation to take care of your bird.

- **They cause considerable damage:** The beaks of these birds are very strong. Of course, they also love to chew on things. This means that your bird will be able to gnaw through furniture, walls, mats or even make holes in your clothes when you are not looking.

- **They are extremely manipulative:** Unless you learn how to deal with an Umbrella Cockatoo, your bird will easily manipulate you into doing whatever it is that he wants. If not trained properly, they even resort to shrieking or biting to get what they want.

- **You will have to deal with hormones:** Although Umbrella Cockatoos only mate once each year, they tend to have several hormonal changes that affect their behavior to a large extent. A generally calm bird will suddenly become nippy and moody. They may even begin to lash out at you without any incident in particular. And, these birds, the females in particular, become extremely territorial during this time.

- **They are prone to several behavioral issues:** Without proper care and mental stimulation, these birds develop several behavioral issues including plucking and screaming. In some cases, you may even find it extremely hard to find what you are doing wrong. If you plan to have a single bird at home, you need to dedicate enough time every day to your bird. Most Umbrella Cockatoo owners suggest that 3 hours a day is ideal for the well-being of your bird. If you cannot dedicate this much time, it is best that you bring home a pair of birds or do not bring home any.

3. Where to buy Umbrella Cockatoos?

The first thing you need to do is find a breeder or a pet store where the birds are reared in captivity and not illegally imported. There are some common sources where you can bring your birds home from. However, whatever source you choose, make sure that they birds are kept in good condition and are, most importantly, not sold illegally. This can lead to penalties of up to $110,000 if you are not careful about it. Here are some do's and don'ts when it comes to bringing home a bird:

Finding a Breeder

In the recent past, several breeders have come under the radar for being extremely insensitive with their breeding practices. Some have even gone to the extent off removing the hatchlings from nests and selling them off to several pet stores. This is very much like the puppy mills that are considered extremely cruel. You will be able to tell whether a breeder is genuine or not based on the care that is given to the birds. Those who only have commercial interests will most likely be extremely negligent and will keep their birds in filthy conditions. One such breeding operation that was carried on in Washington was even described as a parrot concentration camp. The birds were made to live in conditions that were too cold, damp and filthy.

Here are some reasons why it is actually your responsibility to make sure that you choose a good breeder to source your pets from:

Badly bred birds are susceptible to disease

The birds that are kept in very unhygienic conditions often suffer from several communicable diseases including proventricular dialation disease. This leads to weight loss, regurgitation and depression. These birds can transmit diseases not just to other birds but human beings as well. You can contract diseases like salmonellosis, chlamydiosis, E.coli infection, giardiasis, tuberculosis and many others. It is also very hard to care for a bird that is unwell.

Your bird could be smuggled

Almost every day, stories of birds being smuggled are revealed. The instances in which these birds are smuggled can be really cruel. They are dumped in air vents of a vehicle, in the jacket pockets etc. The industry of smuggling treats these beautiful creatures as mere commodities of trade. If you end up buying from someone who smuggles the birds in, you are supporting the industry too.

Birds are left in the lurch sometimes
With many new and inexperienced breeders, having birds becomes very overwhelming for them. As a result, they may even abandon the birds or even resell them. This is one of the many reasons why animal shelters have several parrots available for you to adopt. Close to 85% of pet owners and breeders will give their birds away because they are unable to keep them. In many states, birds are protected by a strict law of abandonment to make sure that they are not just left out of the cage when owners are unable to take care of them. You see, in captivity, birds do not belong to their natural environment, so releasing them like this leads to death and severe injuries due to unexpected predators.

Finding a good breeder
Not all breeders are commercial and unreliable. Some of them do a lot of research about finding the best breeding practices for their birds. They make sure that their clients get nothing short of the best when it comes to the quality of the birds. Here are a few things that you need to look out for when you are buying a parrot from a breeder:

- **Behavior of the birds:** Umbrella Cockatoos are among the most inquisitive and curious birds in the world. If you notice that the birds in the aviaries are slow to respond, fatigued and dull, it means that they are either unhealthy or lonely and bored. Good breeders will not let their birds go through either one of these stages.

- **The appearance of the birds:** Parrots usually preen themselves well and keep their feathers well groomed. If you see that the feathers are out of place and matted in places, especially near the cloaca, it is a warning sign. Bald patches when it is not molting season, is an indication that the bird may have a feather plucking disorder. The beak and the toes should not have any deformities and irregularities. They should be clean, free from scales and dirt. Umbrella Cockatoos are stocky birds. Instead, if you see that their bodies are too thin and fragile, it is sign of poor breeding practices.

- **The condition of the cage:** Bird cages should be cleaned out on a daily basis. If not, they tend to become very smelly and dirty. If you see bird poop and feathers on the floor of the cage and if the toys are covered in bird poop, it means that basic hygiene practices are missing. Take a look at the food and water containers. If the water is murky and full of poop or feathers, the bird may not be well taken care of. This also makes the birds potential carriers of several diseases that affect people and other birds in your home. The bird that you take home may look healthy but could develop difficult health problems in the future. Be very careful about only choosing birds that are housed in very clean conditions.

- **Recommendations:** If the breeder that you choose is reputed, he will have several people who will give you positive testimonials and recommendations. Your breeder will also be willing to connect you with his or her clients, provided they are breeding good quality birds. You can even visit their clients and talk to them about the challenges of raising a bird and the assistance that the breeder will provide you with during this course

- **Interest of the breeder:** The way your breeder talks to you or interacts with you, shows his interest in the bird. Is he just trying to make a sale or is he genuinely interested in getting the bird a good home for the rest of its life. A good breeder will try to make sure that you are competent enough to take care of the birds that they raised with so much care and caution. Some questions that you can expect from the breeder are:
  - Have you had any birds in the past? Which ones?
  - How much do you know about Umbrella Cockatoos?
  - Do you have any other pets in your home?
  - How will you ensure that your birds get the right diet?
  - What is your schedule like? Will you be able to give your bird any time at all?
  - Are you aware of the potential household hazards for Umbrella Cockatoos such as heavy metal poisoning?

- Is your family alright with having a bird? Are there children in the household?

These questions will tell the breeder about your commitment to the bird and whether an energetic bird like the Umbrella Cockatoo is good for your home or not. On the other hand, if the breeder is only interested in selling you the prettiest and most expensive bird, it is time for you to look elsewhere.

Pet stores for Umbrella Cockatoo purchase

Good quality pet stores are not a myth. Some of them are run by passionate individuals who are interested in breeding certain Umbrella Cockatoo species. They may be interested in increasing awareness about these birds and the joy of having them as pets. You will know that a pet store could be buying from commercial breeders or, even worse, illegally smuggling it with the following signs:

- **The aviary is extremely noisy**: Umbrella Cockatoos stay close to their flocks in the wild. They need the companionship of their flock mates for their well- being. When they are separated from this flock after being captured, they still call out to them very loudly. For several days after they are separated from their flock, these birds continue to cry out to their birds.

  Loneliness is one of the biggest issues with birds like the Umbrella Cockatoos. Besides becoming very noisy, these birds can become aggressive and could even develop issues like feather plucking. That is when the birds begin to look unhappy and unkempt. In a good pet store, birds are usually bred in captivity. They are close to their flocks or sometimes even their parents. If the bird has no flock mate, the owners and the employees in the store take the additional effort to become their flock by spending a lot of time with them and keeping them mentally and physically active.

- **The birds are afraid of people:** Pet stores that care for the well-being of their birds will spend a lot of time with them to make sure that they feel loved. Quite obviously, these birds are very well socialized and will be more approachable. On the other hand, if the birds have been smuggled in or have not been given the attention that they need, they will be aggressive or afraid.

Most often, birds that have been smuggled in will relate to people as a threat to their well-being. As a result, when you approach their cage or try to interact with them, they may just retreat to a corner of the cage. Some of them become defensive and will puff up their feathers or nip at you as an attempt to scare you away. These are the signs that tell you that the bird may be a difficult one to bring home as you will have to deal with several behavioral problems.

- **The employees have no clue about the birds they are selling:** Talk to the employees at the pet store. It is not enough that just the pet store owner has all the information about the birds. The caretakers will be aware of the routine and the requirements of the birds if they have been interacting with them regularly. On the other hand, if they have to work with new species that are just smuggled in or bought from breeders, they may not be able to provide any information about the birds to you. Casually enquire about the diet, the grooming process and other care requirements of the bird. Ask where the bird originates from and other questions about the species. If there is a lot of hesitation with respect to answering your queries, you need to understand that caretakers have no experience.

- **The birds are kept in poor conditions:** The conditions of the cage are very important for you to understand how they have been raised. A dingy and dirty cage is definitely a sign that the birds are not kept in the best conditions. However, in the case of pet stores, the bigger issue is that of overcrowding. Pet stores tend to just keep throwing new birds into the cages or aviaries. They take very little care about quarantining the birds as well.

This means that birds are at the risk of infections, diseases and of course behavioral problems. Umbrella Cockatoos, especially, can dislike the idea of having to share their space with other birds. That means that they will retreat completely or will become extremely aggressive.

Birds catch infections really easily. If the cage is already unkempt and the birds are crowded into these cages, you know that these birds

24

may not be the best addition to your home unless you are able to take extra care of them.

Guarantees for your Umbrella Cockatoos

Whether you are getting your bird from a breeder or a pet store, insist on getting a health guarantee. Normally, pet stores may not give you this health guarantee or certificate but every reputable breeder will offer you a health certificate for the pet that you purchase whether it is a cockatoo or any other animal.

A health certificate basically assures the owners that the birds are free from any diseases or possible pathogens at the time of purchase. However, in case, there is any disease or health problem that occurs in the bird, it will be exchanged for a healthier one or the money is returned to the owner. The guarantee period varies from 15 to 90 days depending upon the species and the source that you obtain your bird from. There are a few conditions that you will have to fulfil in order to make sure that your health guarantee is valid for that period:

- You need to get a Certificate of Veterinary Inspection for your bird with 72 hours of purchase. It is recommended that you take your bird to a licensed Avian vet. It is best that you avoid any vet that is suggested by the breeder. These vets could be in lieu with your breeder. If any issue is detected in this exam, your bird is exchanged immediately or a full refund is given to you.
- In case you have any other bird in your home, you need to get a medical certificate and also the medical history for these birds. They all need to be in good health for your guarantee to be valid.
- If you notice any symptoms of disease in the bird, you must make sure that it is examined by a vet within 72 hours of onset of these symptoms.
- In case the bird dies, you need to make sure that a necropsy is performed by an Avain vet. This should be complete with a histopathy report that is made with 72 hours of the death of the bird. In case these tests prove that the bird died of congenital conditions that occurred before the sale of the bird, your money will be refunded. The bird should not be frozen after it is dead for these tests to be valid.

Normally, health certificates are not issued when the birds are shipped. This is because the process of shipping puts the birds at risk of exposure to toxins and infections. Therefore, it is best that you do not make a purchase from online stores. Unless you have recommendations from people who have interacted on a personal level with these breeders, it is always a risk as you do not really get to explore the conditions that the bird has been raised in.

The best kind of breeders are the ones that follow a closed aviary concept. This concept ensures that no birds other than the ones bred on the farm are allowed there. The birds are not even taken to pet shows where they may catch an infection from other birds. This is a great preventive measure to prevent the chance of any disease in your bird.

You also need to make sure that you take good care of the bird to prevent any health issues. Most often your breeder will be able to help you with tips and information regarding proper care. Make sure you pay attention to this. Keep upgrading your knowledge about your bird to be in touch with latest trends in care and medicine that will make your bird live a longer and healthier life.

Things to know before adopting an Umbrella Cockatoo
Cockatoos can be quite a handful. Not everyone is able to meet the demands of these birds. As a result, several cockatoos are abandoned or surrendered each year to rescue homes and bird adoption centers. If you are looking at bringing a cockatoo home, it would be a great idea to actually adopt one instead of buying one. Not only is this cheaper, it is also a very noble thing to do.

You can check for local rescue homes on the Internet. There are several organizations that specialize in bird adoption. Find one that offers classes and help to teach new pet owners how to take care of the birds that they plan to take home.

When you go to a shelter, check for the quarantining process that they follow. Most of them will have the birds quarantined for 30 days and will also have them examined by a certified Avian vet. Following that, these birds will go through extensive rehabilitation where the volunteers in the shelter will ensure that the birds are properly socialized. Some of them may even appoint a trainer to teach the birds skills like stepping up.

If you plan to adopt a bird, it is recommended that you spend some time at the rescue home with these birds, try to socialize with them and pick one that suits your temperament the best. In fact, many shelters have a few mandatory hours that potential adopters will have to spend with the birds before adopting them.

Rescue shelters know best that raising birds is not that easy. Most of them will only give the birds away to owners who are well educated about cockatoo care. To help you develop a positive relationship with your bird, they have several free classes about health and nutrition for birds, general information about cockatoos, training the birds and several other important aspects of having a bird at home.

Just like the adoption of a human baby, adoption of a cockatoo is also a lengthy process. If you do not meet all the requirements stated by the organization, you may even be denied the opportunity to take a bird home. Following is the step by step adoption process:

- The application for adoption should be completed and provided on file.

- Before 6 months of adoption, you must have attended at least two classes offered by the shelter. If your cockatoo has been abused or has certain behavioral issues, the rescue shelter may ask you to attend more classes as well.

- You should visit your bird at least 3 times before you apply for adoption. Your interaction with the bird is monitored to see if you need any more coaching and help.

- If you have other birds at home, they need to be examined by an avian vet and should test negative for psittacosis.

- The cage should be approved by officials from the adoption agency.

- An adoption fee of $325 or £150 should be paid. This includes all the medical expenses and the food supplied to the bird until adoption. Some shelters may not charge these fees if they are funded or government aided.

- If you are located more than 150 miles away from the shelter, you will have to drop a special request. This is because the home visit requirements are harder to fulfill if you live far away.

There are a few adoption policies that you need to stick to. If an official on home visit discovers that you have breached them, the bird will be taken away. Here are a few policies that are common to most rescue homes:

- Adopted birds should not be bred.

- Birds should never be taken outdoors without a proper harness or cage.

- These birds cannot be sold to another person under any circumstances. This may lead to heavy penalty if discovered by the rescue shelter officials.

- The environment that you provide should be 100% smoke free.

- Adopted birds should be examined annually by an approved avian vet.

- The diet should be well-rounded consisting of fruits, vegetables, pellets, nuts and grains.

- You cannot give the bird away to someone else if you are unable to take care of it. The bird must be returned to the rescue shelter if there is any issue with keeping it in your custody.

Some of these rescue shelters may not allow you to take a cockatoo home if you have an aggressive pet dog or cat at home. Some of them do not allow birds in home with children either. This is to ensure safety of the child and the bird.

In a period of 12 months, you cannot adopt more than 2 birds. This is to ensure that you do not overcrowd your home with birds you are unable to care for.

4. Are they suitable for homes with children?

When it comes to children, the excitement that the children will have towards the new pet is the biggest challenge. If the bird is startled or caught off guard, chances are that he will attack.

In addition to that, children may be naughty at times and may playfully tease the bird. This does not go down well with the Umbrella Cockatoo and they will bite or attack. It is common for a child to scream when this happens. Now, most of the time, biting is an act of communication as opposed to aggression. When the child calls out in fear, the bird gets a fitting response and will believe that this is a great way to get attention.

If you have children at home who are under 12 years of age, make sure that you supervise all the interactions. Tell the children that they need to be very careful while interacting with birds. Teach them compassion towards their new pets. Discourage any behavior that can scare the parrot. You see, birds do not understand that they are children. If the child is a threat to the bird, he will believe that all humans are a threat and will begin to behave rather badly around them.

A new bird takes a lot of patience from the owner. If you are able to make this period delightful for the bird, you will have a friend for life. They will always love you and will, of course, be extremely entertaining.

5. Are they suitable for homes with other pets?

Cats and dogs are predators by the natural order. That already makes them a threat to your Umbrella Cockatoo irrespective of how sweet and friendly they are towards people.

During the first few days, allow the bird to become aware of the presence of the other animal. Let him watch and observe your pet cat or dog. There must be no surprises later on. Just make sure that your dog or cat does not approach the cage while you are away. Your cat, especially, should not be allowed to climb over the cage.

When the bird seems settled in, it is time for the introductions. While keeping the bird in the cage, you will let the dog or cat around it. Let them sniff and explore. If your dog begins to bark or if your cat becomes aggressive, separate them instantly.

Now, keep doing this until your dog or cat is used to the bird. That will make them ignore the new member of the family even when in the same room. When you have reached this stage, it may be safe to let the bird out and interact with the pets

You can take this liberty only when your dog or cat has been trained well to heel. When these animals are trained, the risk to the bird is reduced to a large extent as you will be able to control your cat or dog even if they just get too excited.

If you see that your pet cat or dog is chasing the bird around, you must put the bird back in the cage. In case your bird is not hand trained, wrap a towel around his body and your hands while handling him.

In any case, it is never advisable to leave the bird alone with your pets. While they may seem to get along with each other perfectly well in your presence, do not take any risks.

A dog can seriously harm the Umbrella Cockatoo with a simple friendly nibble. At the same time, your Umbrella Cockatoo can rip the dog's ear right off when provoked. As for cats, the biggest threat is the saliva of the cat which is poisonous for an Umbrella Cockatoo.

Remember that you are dealing with highly instinctive creatures. You can never be sure of when their instinctive behavior will kick in. So, it is best that you let them interact in your presence. In case there are any signs of aggression, it is best to keep your Umbrella Cockatoo confined in the presence of the cat or the dog.

6. Are they suitable for homes with other birds?
The first step to introducing new birds is to have the bird quarantined for 30 days at least. This gives you enough time to observe the bird for any signs of infection that could be contagious. To quarantine the new bird, you need to keep him or her in a separate cage, in a separate room. Birds will get acquainted with one another thanks to their loud calls. So, you can expect your pet birds to be ready for a new member during the introduction.

It is never a good idea to place birds of different sizes in the same cage. The larger bird might become more dominating, putting the smaller bird at great risk. If you have an aviary with birds about the same size as the Umbrella Cockatoos such as the Cockatoo, you could keep them together. However, there is no guarantee that your birds will be friendly with each other and will take to each other's company.

During the actual introduction, you will introduce your Umbrella Cockatoo to the least dominant bird in the flock. You can first start by placing them in separate cages side by side. You can also get a new cage that they both can be placed in, in order to reduce territorial behavior. If the birds just mind their own business and do not attack one another, you can consider it a successful introduction. You can progress to the more dominant birds in the same fashion.

These introductions will only happen in your presence so that you can observe the behavior of the birds. When you are introducing the more dominant birds to your Umbrella Cockatoo, it is best to do it in a more open space like the living room. This gives the bird ample room to run away or fly away if there is any sign of aggression from the other one.

After you are certain that these individual introductions went well, you can place the bird in the aviary. Watch the reaction of the other birds carefully. If you notice that one of them retreats completely, it is a sign that he or she is not happy with the new member in the group. On the other hand, if you see your Umbrella Cockatoo being chased around the cage, he could be in danger of attacks and wounds.

Birds may get along with no traces of jealousy or dominance at times. But if this does not happen in your home despite several attempts, it is not a matter of great disappointment. Sometimes, birds may just not get along with one another. That is when you place them in separate cages and leave them alone.

This ensures that no bird is harmed unnecessarily. You will also prevent a great deal of stress that the bird may go through when he is introduced to another bird who is so hostile or even aggressive in some cases.

7. What should my family know about Umbrella Cockatoos?

When you are bringing an Umbrella Cockatoo home, it is natural for the family to be just as excited as you to welcome home a new member of the family. However, the Umbrella Cockatoo isn't just any pet bird; it is a sizeable bird with great mandible power and several special requirements.

This bird is also highly sensitive and will analyze every situation in your home before becoming a part of the household. So, you need to lay a few ground rules to prepare your family for the bird as well:

- The bird will not be disturbed during its initial days in your home. This includes no teasing, no bringing friends over to see the bird, no parties, no loud music and even no talking to the bird. That way, you can establish a sense of security with the new members.

- One must never stick their finger into the cage even for fun. These birds will bite when threatened. And, the bite will be powerful enough to rip a person's finger tip off.

- The responsibilities of feeding the bird will be divided. Initially, the other family members can be accompanied by the person whose bird it is. Then, they will have to do this on their own. Spending time feeding the bird, especially, helps the bird know all the members of the family and associate them with food which is quite positive. Birds are not threatened by their family or their flock as long as they are part of the daily routine.

- Everybody will learn about the Umbrella Cockatoo in complete detail. They can also attend the basic training class with you if you are adopting your bird.

- No one will tease the bird with large and colorful objects like balls or toys. These things make the bird look at you like a predator and he will withdraw himself from you. They will also make the bird susceptible to behavior issues if repeated persistently.

- Whoever leaves the house last will check all the doors and windows and will make sure that the cage is closed. If there are any other additional measures like separating the household pets, it should be done by this person. The person leaving the house last is responsible for taking all the safety measures with respect to the bird who will be left alone all day.

- Only one person in the house will take the responsibility of training the bird. If you use multiple methods or cues, the bird will simply get confused and will not respond to training effectively. This is usually done by the person who is closest to the bird or by someone who has better experience with training and caring for birds.

- Do not encourage the household pets to attack the cage even for fun. Cats or dogs are natural predators who may cause a lot of harm to your Umbrella Cockatoo. In the case of this large bird, even vice versa is possible, considering the size and the power of this bird.

When you bring an Umbrella Cockatoo home, you need to understand that you are bringing home a highly evolved life form. They understand the slightest changes in their ambience. It is the job of the entire family to ensure that the bird feels comfortable in the house and feels like a part of the flock.

Your family should be educated about the needs of Umbrella Cockatoos to make sure that they are alert in case of any emergency. If nothing else, you need to make sure that they know how to provide first aid for common accidents like bleeding and broken feathers.

The whole family should be aware of where the first aid box is placed and where the supplies for the birds are located. They should also have the number of the vet fed into their phones. This way, you are all on the same page as far as first aid and emergency care is concerned.

The larger the flock, the happier an Umbrella Cockatoo is. So make sure your family can be the ideal and most loving flock imaginable.

8. Are there any laws I should know about?

Cockatoos are exotic birds in the United States, UK, Australia or any part of the world outside their natural environment. We have already established that these birds have strict import and export laws attached to them. Now, even when it comes to owning a bird that has been bred in captivity, there are various regulations that you need to be well aware of. Here are a few things that you need to keep in mind to legally have a cockatoo in your household:

Does it require a bird owners' license?

In some parts of the world, getting a bird owners' license is a must. If you are unsure, you can call your local wildlife authorities and make sure that you fulfil the license requirements, if any. In Australia, a bird owner's license is mandatory. You are required to get a license from the Office of Environment and Heritage to make sure that the species of bird that you are bringing home is being monitored properly. In fact, there are two classes of licenses in Australia. Class 1 license allows you to keep birds that are commonly found in this region and are easy to take care of. Class 2 license is a must for rare species that require additional care. The birds belonging to each class are mentioned in detail. In addition to this, the license is only given to an individual who is 16 years of age or older. Any bird that is kept without the necessary license can be taken away from your home.

Does your lease allow you to have a bird?

Most people do not check their lease or rental agreement before they bring a pet home. This can lead to a lot of unnecessary conflict. If your lease says "no pets", you cannot bring a cockatoo home. It is possible that your landowner will have you evicted for breaching this legal contract. If you are discovered with a cockatoo or any other pet, you will be given a month's notice to leave the place.

There are a few exceptions though. Sometimes, the landowner is aware of the existence of the pet and may not really enforce the no pet clause. This is when you can look for the three month rule which says that if you had a bird in your home for three months or more and the landlord did not enforce the rule, you can continue to stay there with your pet.

Of course, you can speak to your landlord before you get a cockatoo. Sometimes, the no pet clause may only refer to animals like dogs and cats and not birds. They may put down conditions like the bird will have to be removed if it is too noisy. You have to make sure that you adhere to these conditions if your landlord is letting you keep a pet despite a "no pets" clause in the agreement.

Do your neighbors have a say in this?
Yes, they definitely do. In case you bring home a bird that is way too noisy and keeps screeching all day, your neighbors can object to you having a pet at home. Many bird owners have had to face the neighbors and even lawsuits for ignoring complaints about their pets. In fact, in the United States alone, there are over 100 attorneys who are working on pet related lawsuits. Although most cases involve horses and dogs, there are times when birds are involved too.

In fact, poorly trained cockatoos may bite people who visit or may cause injuries to children or other pets. The affected person can and in most cases will sue you. If you lose these cases, you will have to bear all the medical expenses of the aggrieved individual along with paying him or her some reimbursement for the inconvenience caused by your pet.

Are there any limits on how many birds one can have?
In several cities, there are zoning laws that determine how many pets you can own. This law generally does not apply to birds kept indoors. However, it is a good idea to check before you take a chance. If you plan to keep your birds outdoors, especially, you need to check if this is allowed in your city or not.

Zoning rules apply even to breeders. Remember that birds are a large investment. If you do not check the number of birds you can have, you may lose your birds and the aviary. That is a big investment down the drain. In addition to that, if you are unable to maintain your birds, you may even have to cough up penalties for letting them get too noisy or smelly.

Usually, a municipality may restrict the number of birds or pets in an average household to five. This also depends on the space available for the animals and several other factors that ensure the well-being of your animal or bird as well as that of the people who are sharing the neighborhood with you.

These laws about companion animals are enforced by the county or the city. So, these laws may vary tremendously from one place to another. In fact, in some states and cities, there are rules about burying your dead pet in the backyard, too. You cannot have a pet buried in city limits and will have to look for a pet cemetery. These rules include birds of all species as well.

Therefore, when you bring home a bird like an Umbrella Cockatoo that is very protected by the law, it is necessary for you to understand other smaller regulations that determine their status as pets. That way, you will not have to deal with problems like eviction or having your pet taken away from you.

Chapter 3: Making the Bird Feel at Home

Now that you have decided to bring a bird home and have also found reliable sources for the same, the next step is to ensure that your bird is taken care of properly to prevent any health issues or unwanted behavioral issues. It is your most important responsibility to ensure that your bird is well settled in your home and feels completely safe.

This chapter will tell you all that you need to know about providing the right care for your bird from to first day of your bird in your home to housing and feeding requirements of your beloved pet.

1. Ensuring that the bird is settled in

The first day of the bird in your home can be very hard on him or her. The transition from the breeders' or the adoption center to your home can be very strenuous. Umbrella Cockatoos, like any other bird from the family of parrots, dislike change and will be withdrawn and a little scared for the first few days. Here are a few tips to make this transition easy for your beloved new pet:

- When you are driving the bird home from the adoption center or from the breeders, keep your car quiet. Roll the windows up, set the air conditioner up to room temperature and place the cage of the bird in such a way that there are no bumps or movements. If your home is far away from the breeders' make sure that you stop frequently to let the bird relax. Do not talk to the bird or play loud music during the drive.

- Make sure that the housing for your bird is set up before you bring him home. Then, just place the door of the transfer cage towards the door of the bird's new home and wait for him to walk in.

- Make plenty of fresh water and food available to the bird. In case your bird has been on a seed diet at the breeders' do not try to change it right away. You can make the changes after the bird is accustomed to the new environment. In the meanwhile, it is alright to introduce a few fruits and fresh vegetables to your bird and see how he responds.

- The cardinal rule on day one is to leave the bird alone. Let him try to understand his new surroundings first. He will most probably not even allow you to handle him. This is natural as your bird has still not formed that bond with you.

- It is tempting to show off a bird as beautiful as the Umbrella Cockatoo. You can invite a friend or two over to just observe the bird from afar. Even if you have people who are experienced with birds, make sure that the Umbrella Cockatoo is not handled by them. That will make the bird anxious and uncomfortable.

- Sleeping might be an issue as the sights and sounds of your home are new for the bird. Make sure that he is away from the television that can keep him up for longer hours. Placing a cloth over the cage will give your bird a nice resting spot.

- Do not interact too much with the bird on the first day. A hello in the softest voice possible is the only thing you can do. Never tower over the cage. Instead, stay at eye level with the bird at all times. This makes them feel like an equal and not like a prey animal.

Allow the bird to just observe you and your family for the first day. The lesser you interact with him, the better it is. You can even ask the breeder to give you a favorite toy of the bird to take home with you. This is a familiar object that will help the bird calm down. The time that a bird takes to open up to you and become more interactive depends entirely on the personality of the bird.

The first week is one of the most important bonding periods with your bird. So do not rush your bird to meet friends and family yet. You have 20 odd years to do that with your bird! Take this time to make your bird feel secure in your presence. Ensure that every interaction with your bird in this time is positive and enriching for the bird. You do not want to make your bird feel overwhelmed at any cost.

This is the time when you unleash the curiosity in your Umbrella Cockatoo. If your bird cage is small enough, walk him around the house and in a very soft voice tell him where he is. You can wait for a day or two if you have to transfer him into a travel cage to take him around. Let him feel the ambience of your home and start to feel like he is a part of it too.

If your bird is young, you need to make more time for him. You see, you are not just a companion but also a parent that this bird will actually learn from. You will train the bird, teach him or her to become more independent and even cuddle a little from time to time. Now, how the experiences of a bird turns out in your home depends entirely on the kind of attention that you give him. There are three *kinds* of attention that you need to give your bird:

- Focused attention: This means that all the time you spend with your bird is with complete attention to your bird. It is a one on one session with no distractions. There will be no television, other people from the household or even your mobile phone. This session is meant to educate your bird and train him instead of just playing with him.

- Ambient attention: This is when you and your bird are hanging out. You could be playing with new toys, using treats to get the bird to move around the cage etc. This is when you teach the bird to entertain himself even when you are in the room. This is when you lightly pet or stroke the bird occasionally while you continue with your routine such as reading or watching television.

- Casual attention: This is similar to ambient attention but you are a little more involved. Allow your bird to play with new toys and explore them. You will also engage in this activity and constantly encourage the bird. This is very necessary for you to develop a good bond with your bird and even keep him relatively independent.

For the first few weeks, you need to make sure that your bird gets an equal proportion of each type of attention. If one is more than the other, it affects the behavior of the bird. For example, if you give him too much focused attention, he will never learn to entertain himself. Instead, he will start screeching or even plucking his feathers when you are not in the same room as him.

It is advised that you restrict this attention to about 20 minutes every day. Once you start training your bird, make sure you establish a routine and stick to it. Preferably, this routine needs to be established from day 1. You need to fix a time to feed the bird, interact with him, train him etc. Cockatoos work really well with routines.

One thing you need to know with Umbrella Cockatoos is that they are slightly rebellious. They love to challenge authority from time to time just to see how far they can get. Especially with the juveniles, you can expect them to try to push the rule and routine that you have set for them. They may try biting or nipping and other such behavior. This is when you need to be extremely firm and tell them that you are boss.

Some cockatoo owners will recommend that you have the height of dominance with your bird. This means that you will never keep your eye level below the eye level of the bird but will always keep it above it. That is never a good idea because your bird may not interact comfortably with you because they will begin to see you as a threat. Instead, you should always stay at your bird's eye level so that he understands that you are a friend or an equal who means no harm. This is the best way to establish trust with your bird.

Here are a few rules that you must follow for the first month of your bird's time in your home:

- The diet should not be changed for at least a month from the time you bring the bird home. Any change will be made gradually by adding small proportions of the food that you want to give your bird with the food that he is already used to eating.

- Rules should be consistent. While you are trying to discipline your bird, being disciplined yourself is very important. If you slack, your bird will know that you are not firm enough and may not adhere to rules set by you.

- Do not have too many people over in this time. For the first month avoid parties as much as you can. It will only make it harder for the bird to get used to his new home.

- Find a time when you are relatively free at work to bring the bird home. If you know that a certain month is demanding at your workplace and requires you to travel or spend long hours at the office, put your plans to bring a bird home on hold. This is a time when you cannot make any compromises on the time you spend with the bird.

2. Providing proper housing

Housing an Umbrella Cockatoo is a challenge owing to the sheer size of the bird. It isn't enough to just build a cage for the bird and leave him there. There are several factors that you need to consider in order to keep the bird comfortable in your home:

The depth of the tail and the wingspan: Your Umbrella Cockatoo should be able to stretch in the cage easily. The wingspan of the bird is about 3-4 feet in length on average. The minimum size of the cage should be such that your bird is able to spread his wings without touching the sides of the cage. The tail is also long, so you have to make sure that it does not get entangled in the bars of the cage.

The minimum size requirement for an Umbrella Cockatoo cage is a depth of 30 inches, height of 60-72 inches and a width of 48 inches. If you are able to get a cage that actually allows your bird to fly, it is called a true flight cage. This would ideally be about twice the size of the dimensions mentioned above.

In the case of Umbrella Cockatoos, the most important factor is the depth. Most breeders recommend that the deeper the cage, the better it is for the bird, although it makes it hard to handle the bird and reach out. The key to keeping your bird in a deep cage is to train them well to step up.

Styles of cages

Bird cages can be aesthetic additions to your home. There are so many different styles that you can choose from. Depending upon the behavior of the bird and your personal needs, you can choose the

41

type of cage that you will bring home. The common styles available are:

Open top enclosures

As the name suggests, the cage opens from the top. You can add a perch to this open end to allow your birds to perch and get a good view of their home. They can even enter the cage easily whenever they want water or food. This style is not suitable for birds that are not trained to step up as you will not be able to get the bird out of the perch to put them back in the cage and close it for the night. Of course, this type of enclosure is of no use when you have a pet cat or dog at home as you can never leave the cage open with the perch.

Playtop enclosures

These play top cages come with a detachable top that you can even use to train your bird. They are similar to the perch of an open top cage. The difference is that the access to the cage is from another place. It could be from the front or the side of the cage. Once your bird has been trained, it is a great space for your bird to play and stretch if the enclosure is not so large.

Solid top enclosures

These are the most common types of enclosures that you will find. The top of the cage does not open and cannot be used as a play area for the bird. This is usually preferred by owners who are not very tall to access the bird from the top of the cage. It is easier to access and of course, easier to clean. When you buy solid top cages, make sure that you get one which is rectangular or square in shape. The rounded ones do not allow free movement for the birds.

Accessories in the cage

A bird cage does require some basic accessories besides the toys. The two most important ones are:

- **Food and water bowls:** Make sure that you get either steel or porcelain bowls for your birds. They should be shallow enough for your bird to reach out and eat or drink from them. If it seems like too much of a struggle, the bird may not eat or drink at all!

  Keep these bowls near the cage entrance. That way, it is easier for you to fill them up and clean them as well. You get special drinkers for birds that are almost like bottles for birds. This is not a necessity unless your vet advises you to do so for an ill bird. It is also important for you to keep a drinker for your bird if you see that he loves to splash around and make a mess. Umbrella Cockatoos love a good bath and will target their drinking bowl even if you keep a separate bathing bowl for them.

- **The substrate:** We know now that birds poop a lot and there should be some substrate that can absorb this poop to keep the cage relatively clean. The best substrate to use for Umbrella Cockatoos is newspaper. It is cheaper, absorbs a lot better and is easier to clean out. Pine shavings or any wood shaving is not recommended as it may be harmful for the bird. If you choose to use wood shavings, having a grate that separates the bird and the substrate is a good idea.

  Ideally, the substrate should be cleaned out every single day to avoid any dampness or chances of infections. In some pet stores, you may also be able to find special bird litter that can safely be used for your birds. If you do not like the idea of using newspaper, this is the best option for you.

Make all the housing preparations well in advance. You can even teach your family about the safe ways to approach the bird cage to avoid being bitten or hurt. The golden rule with Umbrella Cockatoos is to never overwhelm them. Making too much noise or suddenly approaching the bird when he is not expecting you to will startle him and make him react aggressively.

Where to place the cage?

The next challenge is finding a safe spot in your home to house the bird. When you choose a room to keep your bird cage in, make sure that:

- It is away from too much noise. Any room that faces the road or has loud traffic sounds is not a good idea, especially for a new bird. This room should not be the center of the family's activities either. A new bird will feel overwhelmed to see too many people and new faces. Even new voices can traumatize the bird.

- It does not have very bright and direct sunlight. While sunlight is necessary for the birds, if it gets too hot or direct, they may feel a little uneasy. You can even make a "dark spot" on the cage with a blanket to provide your bird with a hiding spot.

- There is a wall to place the cage against. This gives the bird a great sense of security. If the cage is right in the middle of the room, the bird may feel a little vulnerable and afraid.

- The bird is able to observe the family. While the bird should not be right in the middle of your daily activities, he or she should be able to observe the potential "flock". When the bird sees that you are happy in the space, he will also feel secure. Umbrella Cockatoos are very analytical birds and will learn a lot from your body language, the food that you eat etc. Being able to observe you will make it easier for them to trust you eventually.

- Keep the cage away from the kitchen or the AC vents. Smoke or toxins can be transmitted from these areas and can be fatal to your bird. For instance, Teflon fumes are toxic for birds and they should be protected from it.

3. What do Umbrella Cockatoos Eat?

Feeding exotic birds can be quite challenging as you need to make their diet as close to their natural foods as possible.

In the wild, these birds mostly eat several types of nuts and fruits. They also include vegetables in their diet. But, a large part of the bird's diet consists of palm nuts. Of course, sourcing these foods can be quite difficult and you will have to make modifications as required.

It is a good idea to make a mixture of nuts along with the shells to give your Umbrella Cockatoo. This can contain almonds, filberts, Brazil nuts, walnuts, pecans and Macadamia nuts. Macadamia nuts should form the large part of the mixture.

A small serving of these mixed nuts can be given to the bird every day. They are very nutritious, free from cholesterol and give the bird the necessary amount of Vitamin A, Calcium, Phosphorous, Niacin, fiber and protein. Keeping the shell on also allows them to condition their beaks and is a great source of entertainment for the bird.

You will have to keep the regular pellets and the nuts in separate bowls. While pellets do not entirely constitute a balanced diet for the birds, they are certainly a better option than seeds. Of course, these foods do not spoil easily and can be left in the cage all day long.

You must also include fresh produce like fruits and vegetables in the diet of your bird. These soft foods can be given to the bird at about mid-morning. Allow the bird to eat this for a while and when he turns away from it, clean out the food immediately. This food should not be left in the cage for too long.

You need to maintain a certain routine with feeding your bird. The first thing in the morning should be providing the pellets and the nuts. Clean the bowls from the previous day, allow them to dry and add fresh food and water every morning, even if it means wasting a little of the previous day's food. This keeps the cage clean and free from infections of any kind.

Fresh produce will improve the health of your bird. They make the immune system stronger, provide the birds with necessary minerals and vitamins and will also give them a good attitude because they are happy.

Learn as much about bird nutrition as you possibly can when you bring an Umbrella Cockatoo home. This will allow you to make changes in the diet as required and keep the food bowl interesting for the bird.

Fruits like watermelon are great for your Umbrella Cockatoo. These fruits are a wonderful source of Vitamin A, B6 and Vitamin C that maintain the eye health of the bird, fight infections, help curb feather picking in birds and even keep the body free from toxins and free radicles.

Some fruits and vegetables that you can give your bird everyday include:

- Papaya
- Cantaloupe
- Mango

- Honeydew melon
- Kiwi
- Banana
- Blueberry
- Grapefruit
- Strawberry
- Oranges
- Peaches
- Watermelon
- Pomegranate
- Beets
- Pea pods
- Green beans
- Star fruits
- Carrots
- Broccoli
- Green Peppers
- Zucchini
- Yams
- Radish
- Cooked Beans

Whenever you are giving your bird any fruits that contain a pit, make sure it is removed. Even seeds from fruits like apples may have a few toxins that can harm the bird. To be safe, remove the seeds from all fruits while feeding your Umbrella Cockatoo. Never give your bird Avocados as they are toxic to them.

Never give your bird any foods that contain preservatives, added salts or sugars. Choose organically grown foods that are not processed.

If your bird was used to a seed based diet with the breeders, you need to slowly make a transition by adding pellets to the seeds and then increasing the quantity of the pellets gradually. Seeds will make the birds obese and have very little nutritional value.

Since your birds in captivity do not have the joy of foraging, you can make eating time more fun for them by giving them half a cantaloupe or watermelon instead of cutting it into pieces. You can also give them corn on the cob so they can pick and eat from it. This keeps them mentally well stimulated and will make them look forward to eating sessions.

Now, it is possible that your Umbrella Cockatoo will be picky when it comes to the natural fresh produce. It is a good idea to give the bird a range of foods over a few days to see what he likes and what he doesn't. It is best to give the bird the foods that he enjoys. This is because he will not only not eat the food but will also pick at it, fling it around and make a massive mess.

You will also need to observe the amount of food the bird eats and restrict the serving size accordingly. Leaving food in the bowl will eventually lead to a big mess. In the case of supplements in the food, you must never add any on your own, unless recommended by the vet. Some vitamins like Vitamin D can actually harm your bird when given in excess. Even if the supplement is "parrot safe" as per the boxes, it will become unsafe if your bird does not require any additional supplement.

Other sources of foods
- Baby food: Human baby food along with fresh fruits and vegetables makes a great base mix for your bird.

- Dried produce: In case you are unable to source fresh produce, you can give your bird dried vegetables and fruits. In fact, birds enjoy the fact that these foods are crunchy. You also have the option of soaking these foods in warm water. This, it is believed, reminds the birds of the regurgitated foods given to them by parents which is also moist and warm. These foods help birds progress from seeds to a healthier diet option.

You need to make sure that any food that you are giving your bird has no artificial coloring. This is usually done to make foods visually more attractive and can be harmful in terms of nutrition. The other thing to avoid is sulfur dioxide. Check the labels thoroughly to ensure that your foods do not have any traces of this chemical. It may make your bird hyper active, can increase aggressive behavior and can even lead to feather plucking or shedding. Allergic reactions to these additives can have mild to severe symptoms that you need to watch out for.

The most convenient food option for Umbrella Cockatoos is sprouted seeds. This is when you do not have time to prepare the base mix with veggies, seeds etc. An equal portion of these sprouted seeds can be very nutritious. In addition to that, birds simply love sprouted seeds and are a great way to introduce greens to your bird.

Foods that should be given in moderation

- Any veggies that contain many oxalates should be given to the Umbrella Cockatoo in moderation. This includes bok choy, spinach and even chard. This is because the absorption of calcium is compromised with these foods.

- Fruits that contain too much sugar must be avoided entirely.

- Any food that is 100% cooked, including beans, pasta or grains. These foods tend to have more calories and are also high in phosphorous. This puts your bird at the risk of becoming obese.

- Seeds should be provided occasionally or as treats, most preferably. This is because they have very little nutritional value and are high in fats.

Foods that you should avoid:

- Caffeine

- Chocolate

- Alcohol

- Pits of fruits like apricots, plums, peaches and nectarines. This leads to vomiting or even coma as these pits contain enzyme inhibitors.

- Green potatoes, tomato leaves, eggplant. These foods contain poisonous alkaloids. They may lead to diarrhea, vomiting and even difficulty in breathing.

- Raw beans should never be given to Umbrella Cockatoos as it hampers their protein metabolism. In addition to that, it also contains other toxins that can harm the bird. Giving your bird cooked beans occasionally is a better option.

- Nutmeg is a complete no as it contains myristicin which makes your bird nauseous and dizzy. It can also cause vomiting in birds immediately after consumption.

- Rhubarb leaves are extremely toxic to birds. They contain an intestinal irritant, oxalic acid. If your bird consumes large doses of this compound, it could be lethal.

- Do not allow your bird to ingest tobacco fumes or eat the leaves. This leads to seizures, diarrhea and more severe symptoms. Basically, if you are a smoker, you will want to keep your bird as far away from the smoking area of your home as possible.

Umbrella Cockatoos are large birds who need good nutrition and good portions of the right nutrients in order for them to thrive. If you are uncertain about what you must give your bird, you may even consult your vet or an experienced Umbrella Cockatoo owner. But, never assume that what is good for you must be good for the bird. They have different requirements in terms of diet and you need to be careful about maintaining a balance of all the nutrients that they need.

4. Keeping your bird free from danger

This is one of the most important parts of the preparation for a new bird. Before you bring your bird home, you need to make sure that the environment is safe for your bird. Here are some bird proofing tips for you:

- The house should be 100% smoke free. In fact, many people recommended that homes with people who smoke should not have birds as they can develop several respiratory issues.

- Keep the cage away from hard floors or concrete. If you clip the wings of your birds, especially, you have to make sure that the bird will not fall and injure itself.

- Ceiling fans and table fans should be switched off when the bird is out. This is true even when your bird's wings are clipped. Even with wing clipping, a portion of the bird's flying ability is retained. As a result, there are chances that the feathers or wings may get damaged.

- Get covers for all your stove tops or install a door in the kitchen. The kitchen should be a "no access" spot for birds because of the potential dangers in this area. Hot stoves, knives, fumes etc. can be extremely harmful for your birds.

- Cover up all the loose wires and threads. Cockatoos, being the inquisitive creatures they are, will tug at this any may end up injuring or electrocuting themselves.

- Make sure that doors and windows are closed whenever the bird is out of the cage. In case you have a self-closing mechanism for your doors, have them removed and install strong stoppers. You do not want any flight related mishaps due to slamming doors.

- Remove all plants that are harmful for birds. You can consult your vet or can check on the Internet to make sure that none of the plants that you have are hazardous to your pet.

Bird proofing is a must. Although you cannot be 100% safe at all times, taking necessary measures to prevent any accidents is a must. Just keep an eye on your bird when it is out of the cage to be sure.

5. Maintaining the bird cage

It is not enough that you have a beautiful bird cage in your home. You need to make sure that you take good care of this cage and keep it clean to ensure good health of the bird. Of course, no one would want to have a smelly bird cage in their room. There are different frequencies of cleaning for each part of the cage. This is your guide to proper bird cage maintenance:

- **Every day cleaning:** You will have to spend a few minutes each day examining the cage and making sure that it is in good condition. On a daily basis, you will have to replace the substrate that you have placed on the floor of the cage. You will also have to make sure that the food and water bowls are cleaned and the contents are changed every single day.

If you notice any toy with a lot of poop on it, it will have to be cleaned immediately. In case of food that has been spilled, fruits and vegetables should not be allowed to stay on for more than one hour in the cage. Eating a small piece of rotting fruit or vegetable can cause GI tract infections almost immediately.

- **Fortnightly cleaning:** Every 15 days, a complete wipe down of the cage is necessary. Using any antibacterial cleaner that you can get in any pet store, wipe the floor and the bars of the cage. Dirty toys can also be wiped with the same liquid. This cleaning practice must be followed regularly to reduce the breeding grounds for microbes and thus reduce the chances of infection. If the cage is damp, remove the bird from the cage and allow the cage to dry naturally in the sun for a few minutes before replacing the bird.

- **Monthly cleaning:** Whether you have an aviary or just a single cage, this monthly thorough cleaning is a must. First, you need to place the bird in a temporary cage or enclosure. Then, all the accessories including the chains that are used to hold these toys up should be removed and soaked in an antibacterial solution or even mild soap water.

The cage should be cleaned thoroughly. First, any dried feces or debris should be scraped out. Following this, the cage should be washed completely using soapy water. For those who prefer natural cleaning agents, diluted vinegar is a great option.

Make sure that the toys and the cage are rinsed thoroughly to remove any traces of soap. After that, you can allow them to dry in the sun before you replace them in the cage. You will let the bird into the cage only after everything is fully dry.

This cleaning schedule is quite easy to follow and is usually preferred by most bird owners. You will have a clean and hygienic cage that is free from disease causing microbes. In addition to that, keeping an indoor cage clean is a must to keep your family healthy as well.

6. Keeping the bird well groomed

Grooming an Umbrella Cockatoo is not at all a lot of work. In fact, you need to spend a few minutes misting the bird occasionally. This is because birds like the Umbrella Cockatoo groom themselves regularly. These birds do not like to stay messy and will make sure that their feathers are always clean and in place.

However, grooming is an important bonding activity. In the wild, these birds will preen their mates and keep the other's feathers well in place. If you do the same for your bird, he is likely to form a strong bond with you.

How Umbrella Cockatoos groom themselves

The process by which birds keep their feathers in good shape and well-groomed is called preening. With almost 25000 feathers, it is natural for a bird to want to constantly work towards each one of them to keep them in the best condition. This is a behavior pattern that you will observe with just about any species of birds.

There is a gland called the uropygial gland that is found just below the tail of most birds. This gland releases oils that contain natural waxes that help in keeping the feathers waterproof. In addition to that, the feathers also become more flexible with the application of this oil. Each feather is protected and coated as the bird applies the secretions of this gland on each feather.

What is interesting with Umbrella Cockatoos and all parrots is that this gland is absent. Instead, the feathers are broken down into fine power that is applied on the body.

There are several advantages of preening besides making the bird look good. Some of the important benefits of preening include:

- Aligning the feathers in such a way that they keep the bird insulated and protected from water.

- The shape of the feathers is maintained in aerodynamically feasible manner to improve flight.

- Parasites and lice that carry diseases are removed to keep not just themselves but the entire flock safe.

- When the feathers molt, the bird needs to remove a tough coating that is seen on the new feathers. That way the new feathers can be kept in place.

- The bird looks healthier when preened properly and is more likely to attract a mate.

With the bird taking so many measures to groom itself, what could you possibly do to for him? Bathing, feather clipping and toenail clipping are the most important grooming rituals between pet owners and their Umbrella Cockatoos.

Bathing your Umbrella Cockatoo

Bathing an Umbrella Cockatoo is very simple. All you need to do is mist the body of the bird with a spray bottle of water. Only when you see matted feathers should you gently brush the area to remove the debris. Soap is not required to bathe your Umbrella Cockatoo, unless there is a lot of debris that is stuck on the feathers of the bird.

If you do use soap, make sure that it is very mild and that it is thoroughly rinsed off the bird's body. You can even hold the bird under a warm shower. They will enjoy this as it resembles the rain that they are so used to thanks to the rainforests that they originate from.

If the bird turns away from the spray of water and looks uncomfortable, take him out of there immediately. A bird who is enjoying the bath will lift his feathers and turn around to soak the whole body.

Water baths are popular with all breeds of birds. Place a shallow bowl with water and slowly lower the bird into the bath. If your bird is still not hand trained, you can even put a few celery pieces in the water. As the bird forages, he will also bathe himself.

There is a certain season called the molting season when the birds shed old feather and grow new ones. This is a very uncomfortable phase for the bird as his skin will be highly irritable. To fix this, you can give the bird a good misting with a spray bottle. You can use water that is at room temperature to ease the discomfort.

Wing and toenail clipping

Many people advocate against wing clipping. However, in many cases owners find it easier to manage the bird when he is not able to fly off. Umbrella Cockatoos are not stopped by cages and if the quality of the cage is not good enough, you may expect several escapes. Even when you are traveling with the bird, keeping the wings clipped is a good idea.

To clip the wings, it is best that you consult a professional if you have not done it before. It will not cost more than $10 or £5 pounds.

If you want to do this at home, it is best to wrap a towel around the bird's body. Then, let one wing come out of the lose end. Cut about 1 cm from the largest feathers that are called the primary feathers. Repeat this on the opposite side and make sure that you cut the feathers equally.

In case you catch a blood feather, you can stop the bleeding with flour. This will not render the bird incapable of flying but will make him get less lift. The wings are used to balance the body as well so cutting feathers on both sides equally is a must.

To clip the toenails, just place your finger below the overgrown part of the nail and file the nail slightly. Do not make it too short as it impairs the bird's ability to climb and hold their food. The nail should only be blunt enough to make sure it does not get stuck to the upholstery around your home.

7. Making sure the bird is looked after when you are travelling

Unless you are moving out permanently, you will probably not have the option of taking your Umbrella Cockatoo considering the legalities involved.

So, you need to make arrangements for your bird while you are away. Leaving your pet with your friends or relatives is the best option possible. If you have other members in your family, of course, there is no problem at all.

54

However, in some cases, when you have no one to take care of your bird while you are away, you may have to look for pet sitting services. The Pet Sitters International is an organization that you can depend upon in order to find the best pet sitting services. They have a list of independent pet sitters or pet sitter agencies that you can contact.

It is recommended that you contact local bird clubs to find pet sitters who have worked for the members before and have taken good care of the birds. Friends and family with birds can also provide good recommendations for you.

Now, when you are looking for a pet sitter, you need to conduct an interview with a couple of them till you can find someone reliable enough to leave your bird with. During the interview sessions, there are a few pointers that you need to keep in mind to find the perfect caretaker for your bird.

- Ask for the pet sitters' experience. They should have some knowledge about handling birds and taking care of them. If you see that your pet sitter is a novice, you should find out whether he at least has birds of his own.

- Ask them what they know about Umbrella Cockatoo and if they have taken care of these birds in the past. The Umbrella Cockatoo is a large bird and has very specific requirements. One should know how to handle the bird at least. It is not the same as a Sun Conure or a smaller breed of parrot.

- Ask if they have birds of their own. Anyone who has their own pets will also be sensitive to the requirements of other people. They will be sensitive and will understand that you need the best care for your bird. They are also aware of basic body language and will be able to communicate better with your bird. A pet sitter is not someone who will just feed the birds and clean the cage. They are literally taking your place while you are away.

- Observe the way he or she handles the bird. If they are comfortable with the bird and are able to manage him or her well, then they are probably quite experienced. They must also be able to calm a bird down when he is excited or aggressive.

- You need to make sure that he or she is capable of handling an emergency. Ask them how they would deal with various emergency situations. If it is close to what you would do, then you can hire this individual without a second thought.

- In your absence, if they have a personal emergency, how will they deal with it? Will they be able to send in a substitute? If yes, you need to meet the person who will be substituting for your pet sitter to ensure that they are right for your bird, too.

Once you have finalized upon a sitter, you need to discuss the cost and the services that he or she will provide. Make sure that you have it all in writing to prevent any confusion in the future.

Get all the contact details of your pet sitter including the phone number and email ID. You need to have access to him or her whenever you need. Make it a point to call every day to keep an eye on your bird.

Provide all the contact details of the place that you will be staying in. You also need to provide emergency contact numbers of friends and family members.

Make a written routine for your sitter to follow. You must even include the number of your vet in this list. Ensure that your pet sitter knows where the food is stocked, how to clean the food bowls and the cage and also where the first aid kit is located.
The first time you leave your bird is the hardest. You will eventually get accustomed to one pet sitter who can take care of all your bird's needs. It is best to find a sitter who will stay at your place and take care of the bird. This reduces a lot of stress on the part of your Umbrella Cockatoo.

Travelling is one of the biggest points for consideration when you bring home an Umbrella Cockatoo. If you are a frequent traveler, do not bring a bird home.

When you have to take decisions like moving out of a country, think about your Umbrella Cockatoo. If your bird cannot go with you, are you willing to put him in foster care? If not, then you will have to make compromises on your travel for this. Only when you are willing to make these sacrifices should you buy an Umbrella Cockatoo.

8. Travelling with the bird

Travelling is stressful when an exotic bird like the Umbrella Cockatoo is also part of it. You need to take several measures to ensure that your bird is safe and is more importantly legal to take to a different state or country.

The mode of transport that you choose is very crucial for the health and well-being of your bird. Each one comes with a set of challenges that you need to take care of before you take your bird with you.

Legal considerations

Almost all species of exotic birds, including Umbrella Cockatoos, are protected by strict rules laid out by CITES. If you are planning to travel with your Umbrella Cockatoo, you need to be sure that you are aware of all these legalities.

First, when you decide to take your bird to another country or state, you will have to check for a permit requirement. Some states will require a permit under the regulations of CITES, while others will require you to take a local permit as well. For example, in the United States, you need a CITES permit as well as a Permit from the Endangered species act. Check for regulations of the Wildlife department in your state, country and the country you are travelling to.

The Umbrella Cockatoo is listed on the Appendix I of CITES. This means that your bird can be taken to another country only under certain circumstances. You will most likely need a permit from the country you are travelling from and from the country you are travelling to.

Your veterinarian is a reliable source of information. He will be able to help you obtain these permits as well. You can check the official CITES website and the websites of the Wildlife departments of the countries involved.

Plan your travels well in advance because most permits take two months at least for processing. If you have to make a business trip urgently, you will most probably have to make alternate arrangements for your Umbrella Cockatoo.

Here are a few things you need to have when you are planning a trip with your bird:

- Proof that your bird was legally obtained. A breeder's health certificate is usually accepted.

- The permit from the respective countries that you are going to travel to and from.

- Completed declaration forms as required in the destination port.

- A health certificate from your vet that is not more than 30 days old.

Take a few copies of your permits just to be sure. You also need to be prepared to be questioned by authorities at both ports to confirm the reason for import or export of the bird. With all the documents in place, you will not have to worry about your bird too much. Just make sure that his wings are clipped to ease the process of customs.

Getting the bird in the car
Most birds are used to travelling by car because they do it so frequently. Some of them simply love this little trip with the family. However, if this is the first time you are going to be talking your Umbrella Cockatoo with you in the car, there are a few things that you must take care of.

First, get the bird accustomed to the ambience of your car. Transfer him to a travel cage and place the cage in the car for a few minutes. You can leave the windows down or can turn the air conditioner on at room temperature. Never leave the bird in a hot car. In many states, this is considered illegal and is viewed as cruelty against the bird.

The next thing to do would be to get the bird used to the movement. Drive around the block and watch the bird's body language.

If he is singing and perched in an erect posture, he is quite unfazed by the movement of the car. He could even get on to the floor if the perch is shaky. But, the body language will be positive.

On the other hand, if your bird is trembling and has retreated to one corner of the cage, take him back home and put him in the his cage with lots of food and water. Try again after a few days.

As the bird get more comfortable, you can increase the distance of your drive. When you are ready to actually travel with your bird, there are a few preparations that you need to make.

Ensure that there is a lot of clean drinking water available for your bird. You must also have fresh pellets in a bowl for him to eat on the way. The substrate should be thick and have multiple layers. Your bird is likely to poop more when he is travelling.

Make sure that you stop the car every half an hour to give the bird a break. He will be able to stop, drink some water and refresh himself. On the way, keep the air-conditioner on at room temperature and keep the cage away from any drafts. Do not keep the window open as it freaks the bird out. Lastly, place the cage in the shade. Or you could put a towel over half the cage as a retreat spot for your bird. The cage should be kept in a way that prevents too much movement.

Avoid loud music. Instead, talk and sing to your bird to make him feel comfortable. When the bird has completed a few trips with you, you won't have to worry about travelling by car as much.

Air travel
Air travel is very stressful for the birds. This is because they are separated from you and are left in a space that is so unfamiliar to them for the entire travel period.

The first thing you need to do is prepare a file with all the necessary travel documents. You will need to keep this handy as they will ask for it on several occasions during your travel.

Book an airline that has good pet travel policies. Some of them will have services like feeding and changing the water for the pets. This is very important to make sure your bird does not get dehydrated during this period.

Next, you will have to book all the transit flights on the same airlines, if any. That way any service or requirement will simply be continued during your travel. With new airlines, you will have to worry about new rules and regulations.

The airlines will give you all the specifications for the travel cage. You will have to get one accordingly. Have several layers of substrate on the floor of the cage. Water should be provided through a bottle-type drinker. Get your bird accustomed to this before he travels or he may not drink any water at all. Only provide pellets to your bird as they are less messy and easy to manage.

A harness for your bird is a good idea. This will help them stay in place in case of any turbulence or disturbance during the flight. You can throw in your bird's favorite toy to make him a little more comfortable.

The bird will have to pass through customs. It is best that you keep his wing clipped so that there are no accidents like a runaway bird in a busy airport.

Even if your bird seems healthy, you need to have him checked the moment you reach home at the destination port. There is a lot of stress when the bird is travelling by air. He could be vulnerable to infections because of this. Of course, you never know how clean the cargo was. So, it is good to have the bird checked as a precautionary measure.

Chapter 4: Training and Bonding

As mentioned in the earlier chapters, your Umbrella Cockatoo will require a lot of time and attention. One of the biggest parts of bonding with your bird is training. Making sure your bird is trained and well-socialized is important to avoid unwanted behavior. It also helps keep the bird mentally stimulated.

Some of these commands are necessary for the safety of the bird as well. This chapter will tell you all about the basic training for Umbrella Cockatoos. Since these birds are extremely responsive to training, you can try new tricks once you've mastered the basic training.

1. Understand the bird's body language

Besides vocalization, Umbrella Cockatoos use their body language to communicate with you. Understanding what your bird is trying to tell you will help you train him better. It also helps you read how your bird is actually feeling. Here are some tips to understanding your bird's body language:

- If your bird is on your shoulder and is constantly tugging on the collar of your shirt, it means that he wants to get off.

- If the head of the bird is lowered while the wings are lifted slightly, he wants you to pick him up.

- If the bird is hanging with one or both feet from the cage, he is in a playful mood.

- If his rear end rubs the table while he walks back, he is going to take a poop.

- All species of parrots exhibit pinning which is rapid dilation of the pupils. This is either done when the bird is excited or when the bird is afraid. You can study the situation to tell how your bird is feeling.

- If the bird is talking, whistling or singing, it means that he is happy and quite content.

- If he is mumbling to himself or is just chattering softly, he is practicing the words that he learnt.

- Loud chatter is considered attention seeking behavior.

- Clicking of the tongue means that the bird is just entertaining himself or is calling you to play with him.

- Growling or hissing is a sign of aggression. There could be something in the room that is bothering him. Removing that object will make him stop immediately.

- If you notice your bird grinding his beak just before he sleeps, it means that he is very happy to be in your home.

- Clicking of the beak when you pass by is your bird's way of greeting you. At the same time, clicking when you are holding him means that he does not want to be handled by you at the moment.

- If the beak is on the ground and the feathers are fluffed, he wants you to pet him.

- If your Umbrella Cockatoo regurgitates, it is a sign of great affection. They do this only for their mates in the wild.

- Bobbing the head is a type of attention seeking behavior.

- If the bird is just rubbing his beak on the perch, he is cleaning himself.

- If your bird is standing upright with his weight equally on both feet, he is content and happy.

- If the posture of the bird is upright and he is looking at you, it means that he wants you to pick him up right that instant.

- If the bird is feeling restless and impatient, he will rock back and forth on the perch.

- If the bird is standing on one foot, he is relaxed.

- If he is standing on one foot with all his feathers fluffed, he is happy.

- If your bird is standing on one foot and has the beak tucked beneath the wing, he is just cleaning himself.

- If he is standing on one foot but is grinding his beak, he is tired.

- If he is standing on one foot with glazed eyes and semi-fluffed feathers, it means that he is falling asleep.

- If the bird is scratching the bottom of the cage, he wants you to let him out.

- Tapping of the feet indicates that the bird is trying to protect his or her territory.

- Ruffled feathers can mean one of the following things:
  - The bird is feeling too cold and is trying to warm himself up.
  - The bird is trying to relieve tension and stress.
  - The bird is sick.

- If the crest is lifted, the bird is excited.

- If the crest is puffed up it is seen as a sign of aggression.

- If the crest is flat on the ground while the bird is hissing, it means that he is scared or just getting ready to attack someone.

- If the tail is shaking, the bird is preparing for some fun times ahead.

- Tail bobbing means that the bird is tired or is catching his breath after strenuous physical activity. If this behavior is seen even when the bird has not done anything physically demanding, you need to take him to a vet immediately.

- Fanning of the tail is usually a sign of aggression. The bird is displaying his strength through this body language.

- Flapping of the wings is an attention seeking behavior.

- Flipping of the wings could indicate one or more of the following:
  - Pain or discomfort
  - Anger and aggression
  - A call for your attention.

- If the wings of your bird are drooping it is generally a sign that the bird is unwell.

- If the head is turned back and tucked below the wing, your bird is asleep.

- When the head is lowered and turned, your bird finds something very interesting.

- If the head is down and the wings are extended, your bird is just stretching or yawning.

These simple behavior patterns will help you choose the best time to form that bond with your bird. Responding aptly to this body language also helps the bird trust you more because you are one of his own now.

2. Basic training

The two things that you must include in basic training are step up training and target training. Step up training can even save your bird's life. For instance, if you need to remove your bird from a situation that is potentially dangerous, he must respond by hopping on to your finger or arm. Here is how to teach your bird these two important things:

Target Training

Target training gives your bird something to look forward to while performing the tasks that you want him to. Target training is the best way to get your bird to do the most basic thing; getting in and out of the cage.

Give your Umbrella Cockatoo a target that he can follow. This is most likely a treat at the end of a stick. Hold it out to the bird and allow him to take the treat. If your bird does not respond to the target initially, you can gently touch his beak with it and see how he reacts. If it is treat that your bird likes, he will go for it immediately.

Then, gradually increase the distance between your bird and the target and watch him walk up to it and take a nibble. You can then move the target around the cage and see if he follows it.

The next step is to get the bird to follow this target even when the treat is absent. He may do this the first time you present the target without the treat. If the bird does not respond to the target without the treat, then you will have to continue with the treat for a while until he forms the association between the target and the chance of getting a treat with a target.

When your bird is following the target successfully, the next step is to get him in and out of the cage. Open the cage door and hold the target at the door. He will come to take a nibble. Keep pulling it away till the bird is finally out of the cage.

Let the bird explore the area. Make sure it is free from any danger for the bird. If your Umbrella Cockatoo has the slightest negative experience with the first time in open space, he will take a long time to regain trust.

Then, when you are ready to take the bird back into the cage, allow him to follow the target. Finish off with a treat or a toy in the cage so that he associates the cage with only positive experiences.

Step up training

Stepping up is one of the most important things you will teach your Umbrella Cockatoo. The Umbrella Cockatoo is a rather large bird. So, having him step up on a finger can be a little hard. The bird will step up but you may find him too heavy to handle.

The best option is to offer your forearm as the step for a bird like the Umbrella Cockatoo. So, hold the forearm horizontally in front of the bird and place the target just behind your forearm. Then say the cue word, "Up". The bird will go for the target and will step on your forearm to reach out to it.

If the bird does not step up with the target, you can even hold his favorite treat in the similar fashion. Now, you need you keep your hand very still. The bird may nibble at your forearm. However, you must not flinch or move. An unsteady perch is one thing that all birds dislike. He is biting to make sure that this perch will not break. Chew on your lower lip and hold still.

If the bird steps up, praise him and give him a treat. Repeat this a couple of times and then try to just place your forearm before the bird and say "Up". If he climbs up without the target, you have successfully completed your step up training.

Remember that the bird has an additional incentive for stepping up-being with you. They are most likely going to learn this trick faster than any other trick because of this.

Step up training can then be extended to your shoulder or your head. That way your bird can be with you at all times as soon as you are home from work.

Step up training is also valuable in keeping your bird safe. If you are having an introduction session between your bird and other household pets, there could be some signs of aggression. If you notice this, you can get the bird to step up on your hand and take him out of a potentially dangerous situation. Even when you are escaping a natural calamity or say a fire, you can save your bird easily if he can step up faster.

3. Behavior Training

Behavioral issues are extremely common with Umbrella Cockatoos. You can prevent these issues with proper training and socialization. The crux to stopping bad behavior is understanding what causes it. If you have an adult bird, this may be time consuming but it is definitely not impossible. With the right technique, you will be able to manage your bird's behavior quite well.

Managing aggressive behavior

Aggression in Umbrella Cockatoos is usually an attempt to seek your attention. An aggressive bird will mostly display this aggression by biting. Now, what the bird really wants is your attention. If you scream or shout back at the bird, he will read it as a response. Although it is hard to not scream after a bite from the powerful mandibles of the Umbrella Cockatoo, it is necessary to keep your calm.

If the bird is perched on your body while displaying the aggressive behavior, you can do two things. First, put the bird back in the cage and ignore him till he calms down. Go to him only when he is relaxed and does not attack upon handling.

The next thing to do would be to run while the bird is perched on you. They will feel unsteady and they really dislike this feeling. If you do this every time your bird bites or nibbles at you, he will make an association with the unpleasant feeling and will eventually stop.

If aggressive behavior is a sudden manifestation, then you need to consult your vet. There are chances that the bird is in heat or has some health issue that is making him or her behave in this manner. Also spending time with your bird and giving him a lot of attention will reduce aggressive behavior.

Managing screaming

It is a natural thing for your Umbrella Cockatoo to scream for a few minutes at dawn or dusk. This is their natural way of calling out the flock. While this behavior is acceptable, screaming becomes an issue when it is persistent.

If you notice that your bird is screaming every time you leave him alone, he is only doing this for your attention. The more attention you give him when he screams, the more he is likely to continue the behavior.

When your bird screams, leave the room without any response. If you shout back, he will believe that you are having a conversation with him. This will make him scream even louder.

Come back to your bird only when he is calm. That will help him understand that you will only go to him when he is well behaved. Keeping your cockatoo mentally stimulated will curb this issue to a large extent.

Whenever you leave the bird alone, give him a foraging toy or even a puzzle toy. That will make him independent and less anxious when he is all by himself.

Socializing
For a bird as large as the Umbrella Cockatoo, the owners need to take immense responsibility for the behavior of the bird. Even a friendly nip or bite can lead to severe injuries and problems. And, if your bird causes damage to any third party, you as the owner can even face legal charges.

The first thing that you need to do is to train the Umbrella Cockatoo for basics like stepping up and even getting in and out of the cage. This is when your Umbrella Cockatoo is safe to introduce to your guests outside of a cage. Until you are sure that your Umbrella Cockatoo is through with this training, introducing them to strangers is not the best option.

Actually, as far as your Umbrella Cockatoo is concerned, guests are invaders in their territory. In addition to this when your guest is excited to see the gorgeous Umbrella Cockatoo and approaches the bird, it makes him feel helpless. There is another thing that a guest does- he takes the owner's attention away.

In short, having a guest is a negative experience for your bird. You need to make sure that you make it a fun thing for your Umbrella Cockatoo through positive reinforcements.

So, make sure that your Umbrella Cockatoo is well socialized, especially when it comes to meeting new people. Because these birds are so easy to train, you can follow these 12 simple steps to make them friendly and also more approachable when you have guests at home.

- **Instruct your guest to ignore the bird:** If it is the first time someone is meeting your Umbrella Cockatoo, ask them to avoid even eye contact for the first 30-60 minutes. If your guest just goes for the cage, the bird will think that he means harm. However, let the guest stay in a room that the bird is able to watch over. That will let him understand that this person does not mean any harm and is actually welcome in the flock.

- **Let the bird out:** This should be done only if your bird is used to being handled. Let him out of the cage and let him be. The guest should be instructed not to approach the bird. Let the Umbrella Cockatoo take his time. These birds are extremely cautious which means that sooner or later, they will either walk over to the guest or will come to you to seek some security. This way, the bird does not get any reason to be scared and is more trusting towards new people.

- **Teach the guest to handle the bird:** Once the bird is comfortable to just hang around the new person, you can get them to handle it. Not everyone knows how to handle a pet bird so you have to assist them. Even in the case of people who have had pet birds at home, you need to tell them how your bird likes to be handled. Umbrella Cockatoos are different from pets like dogs and do not like to be heavily petted. It may turn them against the person as they like to be treated with a lot of dignity.

- **Let them pretend to be a perch:** The guest should consider himself a perch that the bird will sit on. So just extending the arm out and finger out and staying still is the best option. They will not reach out for the bird. Instead, you will let the bird go on to their arm or finger. Ask them not to move. Birds like Umbrella Cockatoos hate an unsteady perch. If your visitor is scared, do not force the bird upon them. If the person is scared, the bird will be scared and will certainly react.

- **Let the person cue tricks:** If your Umbrella Cockatoo has been trained to perform tricks, then it is a wonderful ice breaker. When the bird is comfortable enough, let your guest cue the trick. Then, providing a treat for performing a trick gives the bird some reassurance. This is the safest and most fun way to get your bird to meet new people. It is a positive reinforcement plan that is sure to get your bird more interested in new people.

- **Call the bird to step up:** This can happen in the second meeting preferably or whenever the bird is fully comfortable with a person. Now, you will step out of the way and will not hand over the bird to the person. Instead, the guest will cue the step up command. Using a target or a treat the first time is a good idea. It is best to do this after the bird has been cued for other tricks. That makes him understand that the new person will give him treats if he does what he is asked to do. There is no room for doubt when the bird has already interacted to some extent.

- **Petting:** It is good to get your bird accustomed to being petted. But, this should be reserved for when the bird is entirely confident about a certain person. You must guide the person and tell them exactly how your bird likes to be petted. For instance, they may love being scratched on the cheek and may hate being touched on the wing. If the person does the latter, be sure that your Umbrella Cockatoo will never let him or her touch him again. Start by petting the bird yourself first and let the guest join in. Then you can take your hand away and let the guest take over. This comfortable transition will make your bird look forward to new people being around.

- **Pass the bird around:** After your Umbrella Cockatoo is accustomed to a group of people, you can simply pass the bird around from one person to another at intervals. You can even add a resting perch in between where the bird can relax while you entertain your guests. The basic idea is to make sure that your bird is used to many hands. This makes them trust people more and will also make them comfortable in front of a large crowd.

- **Make grabbing a positive thing:** Grabbing basically means holding the bird from the sides of the body. This training is essential as it helps the bird stay relaxed when he is at the vet, when he is travelling by flights or even when he needs to be grabbed and taken out of an emergency. This is at a much later stage only with people whom the bird knows really well and trusts. They will begin by approaching the bird with a treat, holding on to him and then giving him a treat. This tells your bird that hands are not something that he needs to fear.

Your guest can begin by just touching the bird and giving him a treat, cupping the body and then giving him a treat and then proceeding to actually grabbing him. You will get them to repeat each step as many times as needed to make sure that your bird is completely comfortable before you actually get them to progress into getting their hands closer to the bird. Then, being handled becomes a regular activity for your bird and he will not feel scared.

- **Take the bird out on outings:** Plan outdoor activities that involve your bird and a few other friends. It can begin with a family dinner or even a casual visit to a friend's place. This prevents the bird from being excessively territorial as he is on neutral grounds. That will make him less nippy and defensive and the interaction is more peaceful. Don't overwhelm the bird by taking him to party or even a gathering with more than ten people.

- **Take the bird out:** Keeping the bird in the cage and going out for a stroll in the park has also helped many Umbrella Cockatoo owners who claim that this helps the bird make observations and even be calmer in front of strangers as they are accustomed to new faces. There may be people who will ask you if they can handle your bird. If you think that your bird is not aggressive, then you can instruct them to handle the bird safely. Only if they follow your instructions completely will you let them handle your bird.

- **Uncontrolled interactions:** Once your bird is comfortable around people, let the interactions be less controlled. If there is a way you would recommend your bird be handled, let the person do just that. If the bird is harmless, he will only freak out momentarily and will get over it very soon. This makes them more robust and will not require you to intervene and protect him at all times.

No matter what you do, never predict how your bird is going to react in any situation. The last thing you want to take for granted is the temperament of your Umbrella Cockatoo. Remember that these birds are extremely intelligent and sensitive and will analyze each situation they are put in. Be around for all initial interactions and when you are certain that your bird is comfortable, let go slowly.

Dealing with Feather Plucking

Feather Plucking
Feather plucking is common in birds, as they use the beak to groom and preen themselves often. The only time it becomes a serious issue is when the bird is actually mutilating himself in the process of plucking the feathers out. The more frequent the feather plucking, the higher the chances of the bird injuring himself. Although it is commonly termed as a behavioral problem, there are several reasons why birds begin to pluck their own feathers, such as:

- Malnutrition
- Cysts on the skin
- Parasitic infections
- Stress
- Boredom
- Cancer
- Liver disease
- Allergies to food or dust
- Inflammation of the skin
- Skin infection
- Heavy metal poisoning
- Metabolic problems
- Dryness in the skin
- Low humidity
- Lack of proper sunlight
- Any disturbance in sleep patterns
- Presence of preservatives or dyes in the food.

You may think that a bird resorts to feather plucking only when he is bored or unhappy. However, even if your bird is too exhausted with

72

little rest, he may begin to pluck his feathers out. A bird who has the problem of feather plucking will be rather aggressive and anxious. This may be very different from the normal demeanor of your beloved bird.

Most often, birds will suddenly display feather plucking when they are ready to breed and nest.

This is also called brood patch plucking. You know that your bird is plucking due to the breeding instinct because the feathers from the abdominal region and the chest area are plucked out. This is actually done by females to be able to transfer heat during the incubation phase. If your bird is not mated, sexual urges make them pluck their feathers as they are unable to fulfil this need. Now, if your Umbrella Cockatoo is bonded with only one person in the house, it is possible that the bird thinks of that person as the mate. When the bird's "mate" showers attention on someone else, say another pet or a new baby, feather plucking is observed.

If your bird is housed in a cage that is too small or if the perch is not comfortable, he may begin to pluck his feathers out. This is because he probably feels uncomfortable and unhappy in his space. If your bird is unable to get enough exercise or mental stimulation, he will chew on his own feathers as an attempt to keep himself entertained.

If you have trimmed the wings of your bird incorrectly, he will begin to pluck his feathers as an attempt to make the feathers more even. Umbrella Cockatoos are very sensitive creatures. If they see a lot of emotional turmoil in their home such as constant fighting, they tend to develop anxiety. Even the smallest change in the environment such as the flickering of a light can irritate the bird enough to cause feather plucking.

This can be a really frustrating time for you as well as the bird and he may develop habits like chewing, biting, over preening etc. In order to curb this issue you need to be extremely patient with your bird and first get to the root of the problem. Understand why the bird is behaving in this manner. If you are unable to figure that out for yourself, you can also visit the vet for a consultation. There are some measures that you can take to help alleviate this issue:

- Keep your bird mentally stimulated

- If he is plucking for attention, make sure that you do not give in to it. Instead, giving him a time out when he starts plucking tells him that plucking does not get your attention.

- Make sure that the food you give your bird is healthy and adequate.

- Get the feathers clipped by a professional.

- Make sure you have regular health checkups for your bird.

- The day and night lighting should be consistent. If your bird is in a room that has a TV, you might want to give him a sleeping tent so that he can get enough rest.

The problem with feather plucking is that it is not easy to fix. Your bird will always have a tendency to pluck once he begins. Also, the rate of feather plucking and the duration depends on the cause. For example, if it is because of an infection, you can give him medicines and feather plucking will subside eventually. However, if feather plucking occurred after you got married and your bird is jealous of your spouse, it may take a lot of time for him to give this habit up. On your part, you need to be patient. If you feel like you are unable to help your bird, you can look for assistance from your avian vet. Follow all the instructions precisely and it is possible that your bird will recover soon. The best remedy for feather plucking is preventive care and ensuring that your bird is always healthy and happy.

Chapter 5: Breeding Umbrella Cockatoos

This is a very common hobby among those who own pet birds. It does involve a lot of work, however. If you do not want to breed your pet cockatoo, all you have to make sure is that your bird does not form any pair bonds and that you do not provide the necessary breeding conditions.

With Umbrella Cockatoos, you will have a long wait before your bird is ready to breed. These birds usually breed when they are 6 years old. As mentioned before, the parents usually provide care for only one of the hatchlings which means that you will have to take over as the parent for the rest of the birds.

1. Looking for a suitable mate

In case you plan to breed an Umbrella Cockatoo, it is best that you bring home a pair right in the beginning. Your breeder will be able to sell paired birds to you. That reduces the stress of introducing birds and hoping that the bird finds a mate. There are three types of pairs that are generally sold:

- **Proven Pair:** These birds have produced a clutch of eggs at some time of their mating period.

- **Producing Pair:** These birds have recently either laid a clutch or have raised their own young.

- **Bonded pair:** These birds are just compatible and have shown mating behavior towards each other but have not reproduced yet.

The proven and producing pairs are usually more expensive than buying birds of the opposite gender separately. This is because, the former are likely to breed faster.

When you are choosing a mate for your Umbrella Cockatoo, it is best to go back to the same breeder because you have an idea about the quality of raising the birds. If you are going to a new breeder, however, make sure that the bird you get home is healthy. You need to make all the enquiries that you make while choosing a new bird for your home.

You can even ask your breeder to help you find a partner for your bird. This may involve your bird spending a few hours at the breeder's aviary to see which bird he is most compatible with. Of course, your breeder will take the necessary quarantining measures to ensure that your birds are nothing short of perfect in health.

The bird that you choose should be tested by a vet. It is a good idea to have a proper physical test, complete blood count and a culture test done in order to determine any potential risks to your bird or to the flock in your home. Of course, the bird should look well physically with all the feathers in shape, the beak smooth and shiny and the legs free from any growth or issues.

When you bring your new bird home, you need to be extremely cautious while introducing them to one another. Make sure you introduce them in a neutral territory to ensure that your pet bird does not get too dominant.

Quarantining is a must with a new bird. A 30 day quarantining process is required. Keep the bird in a separate cage in a separate room for this period. If the bird shows no signs of illness, it is safe to shift the cage of the new bird to your pet's room.

Make sure you monitor the first few interactions to ensure safety of either bird. If they growl, display fanning of the tail feathers or are aloof, put them back in their respective cages and introduce them again.

Only when the birds get used to one another should they be allowed to be in one cage. You will need to keep them in a new cage to avoid any chances of territorial behavior. Observe the birds. You can start off with a few hours in the same cage and gradually increase the time.

When your birds are in heat, the natural progression is for them to mate with one another. They will begin to show very distinct mating behaviors. The male will lower his head and will spread open the wings in an attempt to woo the female. He will also preen her feathers and will feed her. The female reciprocates with the same type of behavior.

This is when you need to begin preparing for the breeding season as mentioned in the section below.

2. Providing the right breeding conditions

If birds do not have the right conditions for breeding, they may not breed at all. The two most important factors are the nesting box and the diet. Here are all the details that you need about both these conditions.

Setting up the nesting box

Once you have a compatible pair, you can set up a nesting box during the breeding season. It is a good idea to put this box outside the cage. If you have pets at home, you will have to put the birds away in a separate room that remains closed. The box is typically wide and deep. This gives the birds room to move around. A deep box mean that the birds will not take the nesting material out. With Umbrella Cockatoos, they will exhibit nesting behavior and will try to hoard all thread-like items in this box in an attempt to build a nest.

It is best to get a box that is made of wood. Wood helps the birds stay warm, as opposed to metal that can get cold. When the incubation period arrives, wood also retains moisture. The advantage with metal ones is that they last longer and are easier to clean. Make sure that the nesting box is secured tightly.

The opening for this box should be on top. If you provide a wooden nesting box, your Umbrella Cockatoos will chew them and modify them a little. Having a trap door at $1/3^{rd}$ the height of the box allows you to access the nesting box to feed the birds or remove the babies when the time comes. To help the birds climb in and out of the box, add a wire mesh strip from the top of the box to the bottom. This acts as a ladder.

You can fill the nesting box almost all the way up to the opening with pine shavings. You can also use shredded newspaper. The birds will take out all the unwanted nesting material.

Diet

You need to give your bird a good diet to stay healthy during the breeding season. The female may require calcium supplements to ensure that the egg shells are intact. In case your bird is still not on a full pellet diet, this is not the time to wean him. You will give the bird the regular diet to prevent any stress. You can just add vitamin mineral supplements to their diet and even give them a cuttlebone to chew on.

Adding assorted nuts to the diet will help the bird to a large extent. Each nut has specific functions that aid the breeding season. Here are a few nuts that you should include and the benefits of these nuts:

- Macadamia nuts- They provide the additional fats that are required in a bird's diet during this season.
- Walnuts- They provide the birds with necessary omega 3 fatty acids.
- Filberts- They are a great source of calcium for the females.
- Pistachios- They aid vitamin A in large amounts.
- If your bird is already on a pellet diet with fresh produce, you only have to worry about giving them the pellets recommended for the breeding period. No added supplementation is necessary with pellets as they are already fortified. You can place a cuttlebone just in case and the bird will chew on it if she needs the calcium.

3. Egg laying

After about 25 hours of the fertilization of the egg, the female will lay the first egg. She will lay about 2-3 eggs, laying one each day. She will have a second clutch of eggs after a month. If you want the bird not to lay the second clutch you can reduce day time to about 10 hours. You can move the birds to a dark room or could just turn the light off early. Just when the bird is about to lay the first egg, her droppings become smelly and large. She will also show evident abdominal distension.

If you see that the hen is leaving the eggs dormant without sitting on them, you will have to increase the temperature of the nest using an aquarium heater. Parrots are known for abandoning their clutch. If you see that your bird does not sit on the eggs and incubate them

78

even after increasing the temperature, you will have to incubate the eggs artificially.

If the hen does brood, the incubation period is about 28 days.

4. Artificially incubating the eggs

To incubate the eggs, you can purchase a standard incubator from any pet supplies store. You can also order them online. It is never advisable to prepare your own incubator, as the temperature settings need to be very accurate to hatch the eggs successfully. The incubation period will be the same as the natural incubation period.

The incubator is a one-time investment that is completely worth it if you choose to breed more Umbrella Cockatoos even in the next season.

Here are a few tips to incubate the eggs correctly:

- Pick the eggs up with clean hands. The chicks are extremely vulnerable to diseases and can be affected even with the smallest traces of microbes. Only pick eggs that are visibly clean. If there is a lot of debris or poop on a certain egg, it is best not to mix it with the other eggs as it will cause unwanted infections.

- Wash the eggs gently to clean the surface. The next step is to candle the eggs. This means you will have to hold the egg up to a light. If you can see the embryo in the form of a dark patch, it means that the egg is fertile. On the other hand, if all you can see is an empty space inside the egg, it is probably not going to hatch.

- In the natural setting, the eggs are usually given heat on one side while the other side remains cooler. Then the hen may turn the eggs with her movements. It is impossible to heat the egg evenly even if you have a fan type incubator that heats up the interior of the egg quite evenly.

- The next thing to keep in mind is the transfer from the nest box to the incubator. Line a container with wood shavings and place the eggs away from each other. Even the slightest bump can crack an egg. You need to know that a cracked egg has very few chances of hatching.

- The incubator will also have a humidifier that will maintain the moisture levels inside the incubator. The temperature and the humidity should be set as per the readings advised for Umbrella Cockatoos. That is the ideal condition for the eggs to hatch.

- In case you want to be doubly sure, you can also check the temperature with a mercury thermometer regularly.

- It is safest to place the eggs on the side when you put them in the incubator. They are stable and will not have any damage or accident.

- Heating the eggs evenly is the most important thing when it comes to the chances of hatching the egg. Make sure you turn the eggs every two hours over 16 hours. This should be done an odd number of times. The next step is to turn the eggs by 180 degrees once every day.

- Keep a close watch on the eggs in the incubator. It is best that you get an incubator with a see-through lid. This will let you observe and monitor the eggs. If you notice that one of them has cracked way before the incubation period ends, take it out of the incubator. If the eggs have a foul smelling discharge, begin to take an abnormal shape or change color, you need to remove them as they could be carrying diseases that will destroy the whole clutch.

- Usually, Umbrella Cockatoo eggs will pip after 24-48 hours of the completion of the incubation period.

- The hatching of the egg begins when the carbon dioxide levels in the egg increase. This starts the hatching process. All baby birds have an egg tooth which allows them to tear the inner membrane open. Then they continue to tear the egg shell to come out.

- The muscles of the chick twitch in order to strengthen them and to make sure that he is able to tear the egg shell out successfully.

- Never try to assist the hatching process unless you are a professional. If you feel like your chicks are unable to break out of the egg shell, you can call your vet immediately.

Watching the eggs hatch is a magical experience. You can do a few small things to make your clutch more successful. For instance, if you are buying a brand new incubator, turn on the recommended settings and keep it on for at least two weeks before you expect the eggs to be placed in them.

Make sure that the incubator is not disturbed. Keep all the wires tucked in to prevent someone from tripping on it and disturbing the set up or turning the incubator off. It is best to place this incubator in areas like the basement that are seldom used by you or your family members.

5. How to raise the chicks

Towards the end of the incubation period, you need to set up a brooding box which can either be purchased or even created using a simple cardboard box. This is where the chicks will be raised until they are large enough to feed on their own and occupy a cage. You may have to raise the chicks even after they have been hatched naturally, as Umbrella Cockatoos do not make the best parents.

Now, this box needs to have an internal temperature of 36 degrees centigrade. You can maintain this using a heating lamp. If you do not feel confident to do this, you can just buy a readymade brooder. These brooders have recommended settings that will ensure that your bird is in safe hands.

As soon as the egg hatches, the hatchlings should be shifted to this brooder or brooding box.

Young birds are seldom able to feed on their own. You will have to make sure that you give the birds the nutrition that they need by hand-feeding them.

Your vet will be able to recommend a good baby bird formula that you can feed the hatchlings. All you have to do is mix the formula as per the instructions on the box. Then, using a clean syringe or ink dropper, you can feed the babies.

When you are feeding the bird, make sure that you place him on a towel because this is going to be a rather messy task. Then hold the head of the bird between two fingers and push the upper jaw gently. The bird will open his mouth automatically. Then, you will have to hold the syringe to the left of the bird's mouth or to your right and then let the food in. This ensures that your bird does not choke on the food that you are giving him.

When the birds are done eating, they will automatically refuse the feed. You will have to feed hatchlings at least once every two hours. Make sure that you watch the body language of the bird. If he is resisting the feed, you can wait a little longer and then do the same.

As the birds grow, the number of feeding sessions will reduce. Ideally, by the time the feathers of the birds appear, they will be feeding about three times every day.

The next step is to wean the birds or make them independent eaters. This can be done when the birds are about 7 weeks old. You can introduce solid foods like pellets and fruits to the bird along with the handfed formula.

Just place a few pieces of fruit or some pellets in front of the bird and wait for him to taste it. If he likes it, he may eat a little and then move on to the formula. Try introducing different fruits and vegetables and notice which ones are tempting enough for the bird to leave the formula for.

You can replace one meal with the favorite food of the bird and add a few pellets too. You will notice that eventually the birds will eat when they are hungry and will not accept the hand fed formula. That is when they are fully weaned.

Incubating the egg artificially has several advantage. To begin with, it encourages the parent birds to lay another clutch of eggs. Next, it increases the chances of the egg hatching. As for hand feeding, it makes your birds familiar with people and will also make them easier to train. Umbrella Cockatoos are known to be bad at parenting and are notorious for leaving their babies hungry.

On the other hand, when a bird is raised by the parents, they will develop a parenting instinct that is better than that of a hand fed bird. They are likely to be better breeders.

The best thing to do would be to allow the birds to feed the little ones for a while. Then you can intervene and help the babies wean. This is called mixed parenting and is best for those who intend to breed Umbrella Cockatoos commercially.

6. Weaning the chicks
You know that the bird is ready to be weaned when he starts handling small objects with his beak or tries to climb using the beak. You will now reduce the formula to twice a day and introduce the bird to eating on his own. Weaning basically means that you are getting the bird to a stage when he can eat on his own without your help or the parent's help.

Place the babies in a cage that is lined with newspaper. Place a feeding bowl and a water bowl inside. You need one for each chick and it should be shallow enough for the bird to eat from. It is recommended that you put the bird into this cage after hand-feeding in the morning. If the birds are very hungry, they may refuse to eat on their own.

You will be able to attract the babies to the new food, preferably special baby pellets, by mixing in rice crispies. You will see that they do not mind experimenting as long as their tummy isn't fully empty. Eventually they will stop eating in the evening. Then they will slowly take to eating on their own and will wean with time. Never rush the baby. Prepare a feeding routine and stick to it and they will eventually learn to eat all their food on their own.

7. Is hand-feeding needed?
You will have two options to choose from once the babies have hatched. You may allow the parents to feed and raise the babies, in which case the birds are more social towards other birds. The other option is to hand-feed the bird and make them tame. The former are

better breeders while the latter make better pets. So it really depends upon what you plan to do with the hatchlings.

If you decide to hand-feed the birds, the ideal age to remove them from the cage is when they are about 3-4 weeks old. This is when the birds are in their pin feather stage. Their feathers look like quills at this stage. This is the best age as the birds are able to hold the body heat and will not require any artificial heat. These birds also have the advantage of being raised by their parents and will be healthier. Immunity is better as the parents will pass on antibodies while feeding the babies.

Choose a formula recommended by your vet. Prepare the formula as per the instructions on the package. You need to make sure that the formula is heated to about 100 degrees F and not more than that. This can scald the insides of the delicate baby bird.

It is better to use a spoon to feed the baby as opposed to a syringe as you will be able to control the food going into the belly of the baby. That way you reduce the risk of choking the baby. Feeding with a spoon is much slower. So chances of overfeeding are fewer. When the baby is full, you will be able to see the signs that will tell you when to stop feeding. You will also spend more time with the baby when you feed him with a spoon.

In case you pull the babies out of the nest earlier or have to hand-feed them at an earlier stage because they were artificially incubated, you will have to purchase a brooder that will keep the babies warm as you feed them. The formula must be made very watery and should be given to the bird in small quantities. Then you wait for the crop to empty and feed the baby again. At a very young age, you may have to feed the baby every two hours.

In case of the pinfeather stage, you can feed the baby 4-5 times and give him some time to rest overnight. That way the crop will be fully empty and he will be ready for next meal.

Chapter 6: Umbrella Cockatoo Healthcare

Healthcare is one of the most important aspects of having a pet. With Umbrella Cockatoos that are more susceptible to infections than other birds, you need to take extra care to keep the bird healthy. This chapter will tell you in detail how you can provide great healthcare for your birds and also the common diseases that you need to be aware of.

1. Finding a good avian vet

The first step is to find a reliable avian vet. Avian vets are specialists in dealing with exotic birds. In addition to the general veterinary study, these vets work with exotic birds as part of their initial practice. Most of these vets are also members of the Association of Avian Vets. While it is not mandatory for your avian vet to be a part of the AAV, someone who is a part of it has access to several seminars and conferences conducted by this organization.

It is not very hard to find an avian vet given the popularity of birds as household pets. However, the biggest challenge that you will face is finding one close to your home. While the regular vets can be approached for emergencies, an avian vet is a must to deal with particular diseases and problems faced by these birds.

The best place to look for a good avian vet in your locality is to check the Internet. Most of the specialized vets are listed here. The official website of the Association of Avian Vets or www.aav.org will be able to help you locate a good avian vet in your area. The Veterinary Medical Association can be contacted in any part of the world to obtain information about avian vets.

When you do find an avian vet for your bird, make sure that you visit him or her to check out the facility. Once you make this visit, there are a few questions that you must ask him or her to confirm if they are capable of taking care of your bird. Here are a few things you may ask your vet:

- **How much experience do they have with treating birds?** The more time your vet has spent treating birds, the more they are equipped to handle complicated cases. A good background in avian medicine is a must.

- **Have you treated Umbrella Cockatoos before?** The anatomy of birds may be more or less the same. But, the reaction to different birds to various medical procedures can be quite different. Even the symptoms displayed can be very different.

- **Do you have birds at home?** A vet who is also a pet owner will be more sensitive to your bird. They will have better understanding of the bird's body language and will be able to pick up the most subtle signs that the bird may show during the treatment.

- **Do you have any emergency care provision?** Your vet should provide some form of after hours care or should have a tie up with a veterinary emergency facility. This is to make sure that you can get the right treatment for your bird in case of any emergency.

- **Is he willing make house calls?** Sometimes, birds can get really stressed out and will not be able to travel to the facility for treatment. This is especially true in case of any poisoning or injury that the bird has to deal with. Your vet should be able to provide some sort of house call facility. He may personally attend the bird or should be able to send someone over from the clinic.

- **What are the service costs?** This is the most important question to make sure that you are not caught off guard by exorbitant prices to see your bird. Make sure you get a full rate card that talks about all the services and emergency care fees as well.

- **How often are check-ups recommended?** A good vet will recommend at least one check up every year for your bird. They will tell you in detail what procedures need to be carried out on a regular basis to keep your bird in good shape.

When you are at the vet's also ask for the insurance options for the bird. There are a few insurance plans for birds that will cover a part of the medical care offered to the birds. However, bird insurance is not as perfect as insurance for other pets like dogs or cats. Some of them may even provide third party insurance that covers for any damage caused to other people by your bird. Make sure you check all the clauses of the insurance plan before investing in it.

Most cockatoo owners prefer to open accounts separately to take care of any emergency medical needs of a bird. A part of their income is set aside in an account every month. This is more reliable than an insurance because birds do not have foolproof plans that can keep you prepared for any emergency.

2. Identifying a Sick Cockatoo

Many bird owners have spoken about unexpected deaths of their pets. While there are some diseases that have very low incubation periods, most can be detected quite easily at an early stage if the owner is able to recognize the signs of illness in the bird. This is what you need to watch out for:

- Abnormal droppings: The droppings of the bird are the first sign of any illness. The consistency of the poop and its color determine which part of the body has been affected. These are a few abnormalities that you need to keep in mind:
  - Any air pockets in the poop is a sign of gas development in the bird's gut.

  - Droppings which are black or red in color is a sign of egg binding, an infection of the intestine or internal bleeding that may be caused by swallowing a foreign object.

  - If any undigested food is excreted, it shows that the bird may have problems in the Pancreas or has an infection of some sort.

  - Diarrhea or loose stools is a sign of multiple issues like infections, parasites or even digestive issues.

- If your bird has been dropping very liquidy poop for more than two days, it is a sign of some infection in the kidney.

- If the urine content or the transparent liquid part of the poop is less, your bird is possibly dehydrated.

- If the semi solid part of the dropping is yellow or green in color, it suggests a liver condition.

- If the urine is yellow in color, it is a chance of a kidney condition.

- There are fluctuations in the weight: You need to have a gram scale in your home and weigh your bird from time to time. Of course, there are minute changes based on how much your bird has eaten, the pooping cycle etc. However, if you notice that your bird has lost more than 10% of his total body weight, you need to consult your vet immediately.

- Change in physical appearance: You will notice signs like discoloration of feathers, puffed up feathers and dried poop near the vent. There could be other signs that raise caution. Remember that Umbrella Cockatoos are fastidious in keeping their body clean. So, a bird who looks messy is possibly unwell.

- Loss of appetite: Umbrella Cockatoos are good eaters. However, if you notice that they are leaving their food untouched, it is a matter of concern. Even if your bird does not seem fatigued or low in energy, a loss of appetite is a sign of possible illness.

- Withdrawn body language: If your bird retreats to one corner of the cage and spends most of the time on the floor, he is showing signs of illness. In addition to that, the feathers may droop and he may even keep his beak hidden under the wings.

- Discharge of fluids: If you see any discharge from the nasal passage or the eyes, it is a sign of infection. This needs to be attended to immediately.

- Inactivity: Umbrella Cockatoos are extremely active birds. They love to climb, fly and play. If your bird is less vocal or shows a sudden drop in his levels of physical activity, rush him to a vet immediately.

- Cloudy eyes: An Umbrella Cockatoo has beady eyes that always sparkle like they are up to some mischief. But, when they are unwell, the eyes become dull and seem quite cloudy.

These are the most common signs of illness in Umbrella Cockatoos. Of course, they may develop other behavioral problems like biting or fear of people when they are hurt or unwell. Even if it is not illness at all, when you notice the slightest deviation from the normal, take your bird to a vet immediately. As they say, prevention is better than cure, especially in birds that can develop fatal conditions overnight.

3. Common Umbrella Cockatoo diseases

There are different diseases that affect pet birds. In case of Umbrella Cockatoos, most conditions that affect Psittacines will affect them too. In the following section, we will talk about various diseases that affect different parts of the bird.

Skin and beak disorders

The common skin and beak problems with Umbrella Cockatoos include:

Feather cysts

Sometimes, the feathers of the birds are unable to grow out through their skin and will curl up under the skin to make a mass as the feather grows. You will notice lumps and swellings on the skin that look somewhat elongated. Any infection in the feather follicle or any trauma to the skin is responsible for this disorder. You will have to get the follicle surgically removed to ensure that the condition does not occur again in the bird.

Ringworm

This is a condition caused by a fungi called *Cryptococcus*. It normally causes facial dermatitis in most parrots and related species. Caged birds may have other skin inflammations caused by Fungi and yeast when the cage is not very well maintained.

Parasitic infections

Leg mite and scale face is normally seen in birds. The face and legs develop a mange like appearance. It normally starts with the formation of crusts around the nostrils, beak and the eyes of the bird. If not treated on time, it can even lead to deformity in the beak of the bird. These crusts may even form on the toes and the legs of the bird. An anti-parasitic medication is prescribed in these conditions that can either be injected or orally administered to the bird.

Psittacine Beak and Feather Disease

This is one of the most common conditions affecting pet birds. This is caused by a virus called the circovirus. Although the name is beak and feather disease, the condition normally affects only the feathers of the bird and very rarely the beaks.

The first case of this condition was first documented in Cockatoos. Strangely, even these birds only had feather damage despite which the disease was named as such.

This infection is very common in the younger birds and is usually seen in birds that are less than 3 years old. The most common signs are feather loss in areas that the bird cannot reach to pluck them out, abnormality in the mature feathers, lack of powder down and also abnormal pin feathers. The infection can spread rapidly, leading to death in most birds before the condition is even diagnosed.

This condition spreads when one bird comes in contact with the feather dust, feces or dander of another affected bird. Most often it is passed on from the adult to the offspring. Even unhygienic nest boxes can be sources of infection.

It is recommended that you isolate a bird that has developed this condition. In worst cases, the birds are euthanized. The problem with this condition is that there is no cure, only preventive care. Making sure that you follow strict quarantining rules, keep the birds in extremely hygienic spaces and following healthy breeding practices can reduce the chances of the disease spreading within your flock.

Other types of feather damage

Sometimes, your bird will have a very shabby appearance with the feathers appearing chewed or almost moth eaten. This may be due to feather plucking which is common in cockatoos. However, there are several other causal factors for feather damage in cockatoos:

- Parasites like red mite, lice and feather mites can cause severe damage to the feathers of the bird.

- Improper nutrition makes the birds less immune to infections and will also affect the function of various organs that are responsible for good skin and feather health.

- Fungus or bacteria from unhygienic cages can lead to infections in the follicle. This type of infection is usually cured with medicines.

- Organ failure, tumor, respiratory conditions and even liver damage can make your bird feel highly stressed. This leads to either self-mutilation or loss of feathers naturally.

- There are various other irritants like tonics that you use on the plumes, ointments, insect bites or even oils that are secreted on human skin that can cause infections. That is why it is recommended that you either use a sanitizer or clean your hands properly before you handle pet birds.

Nutritional disorders
The diet that your bird follows is one of the most crucial aspects of his health. When you stick to a single source of nutrition like seeds or pellets, you are depriving the bird of several nutrients that can only be obtained from fresh fruits and vegetables. Even fortified bird pellets cannot fulfil the nutritional requirements of birds.

When they do not receive all the nutrients that they require, birds will develop several health issues. You will be able to see specific symptoms for each nutrition related disease that birds may suffer from.

Today, avian nutrition has seen a lot of improvement as the knowledge about the requirements of birds has also increased tremendously. When you give your bird any food, be very careful about its contents. Very often, the preservatives and dyes used in the foods can adversely affect the bird. Sometimes, when you provide the bird with vitamin supplements in the water, they may not even drink it because of the taste and develop disorders related to dehydration as well. Some of the most common nutritional deficiencies in birds are:

Vitamin A Deficiency
Normally, vitamin A deficiency is unrecognized in birds. It is most common in birds that rely on a diet of nuts and seeds. This kind of a diet lacks most nutrients, especially vitamin A. Of course, if you give your bird too much supplementation of Vitamin A, it can lead to some serious side effects too! The common problems related to excessive Vitamin A are bone abnormalities, liver disease and even reproductive disorders.

There are a few minute signs that you will observe when the bird has a Vitamin A deficiency. These signs depend upon the organ that has been affected. In the earliest stages, you will notice various white spots on the body of the bird. These white spots will eventually become painful abscesses.

They can block the lungs or the respiratory tract of the bird, as well. This leads to panting and labored breathing. If left untreated, the bird may even die of suffocation. When the abscess becomes too large, the bird will begin to show a lot of swelling near the eyes. In addition to this, you will notice discharge from the nasal cavity of the bird.

There are other milder symptoms of Vitamin A deficiency as well, including thinness in the plumage, fading of the colors, tail bobbing, lethargy, depression, lack of appetite, bad breath and even gagging.

You can prevent this type of deficiency by ensuring that the diet of your bird is formulated with enough Vitamin A precursors. These precursors are converted into Vitamin A when consumed by the bird. Ask your vet to suggest any vitamin A precursor that is not a potential threat for toxicity.

Never make a supplementation decision on your own. If you are giving your bird a balanced meal but are still seeing these symptoms, consult the vet. Only give the bird the doses of vitamin A as recommended by him. Any excessive dosage can lead to iron storage issues with birds.

Make sure that you include as many natural sources of Vitamin A as you can in your bird's diet. This includes fruits like papaya, cantaloupe, broccoli leaves, turnip leaves, collards, egg yolks, chili peppers, spinach and dandelion greens. They are the safest and most reliable sources of nutrition for your bird.

Iodine deficiency
Goitre is a common condition with birds. The thyroid glands in birds are very small but can enlarge to about thrice their size in case of any iodine imbalance. The most common signs of iodine deficiency in birds include clicking, wheezing and heavy breathing. Regurgitation may also be observed in some birds. Cockatoos that are affected with iodine deficiency have a very poor tolerance to stress.

You can help your bird by adding supplements like Lugol's iodine in the water that the bird drinks. Using pellets that are fortified with iodine may also work very well with your Cockatoo.

Vitamin D3, Phosphorous or Calcium Imbalance
When your birds are restricted to a seed diet, an imbalance in the phosphorous and calcium ratio is also seen. This leads to a deficiency in the amino acids in the bird's body. The ratio of calcium, vitamin D3 and phosphorous is very important because all the vital functions are completed because of this delicate balance.

The biggest problem is providing birds with excessive sunflower seeds because they contain low calcium and amino acid levels. Some pet owners would suggest that you replace sunflower seeds with safflower seeds. This, too, is not the best idea because these seeds are very high in their fat content and may lead to obesity in the bird. They are also equally low in calcium and amino acids.

Vitamin D Toxicosis

While vitamin D is essential to your bird, excessive supplementation causes more harm to your bird than good. This leads to an unnatural accumulation of calcium in the kidney and other tissues of the bird's body. Always consult your vet before giving your bird any supplementation.

Iron storage disease

This is a very serious condition that may damage the vital organs of birds, including the liver and the kidney. Every bird's body needs a certain amount of iron to produce the required level of hemoglobin. This is necessary to transfer oxygen from the lungs to the rest of the body. In some cases, however, when the iron build up in the body is excessive, it gets stored in the liver, the heart and the lungs. When stored in these organs, iron can cause a lot of damage.

Iron storage disease comes with almost no signs. You will only notice the health of the bird deteriorate rapidly a few days before it dies. Sometimes, owners are lucky enough to notice signs like a distended abdomen, fluid in the air sacs, labored breathing and fatigue.

Stress and genetic factors also play a rather important role in the development of this condition in birds. This condition is not only related to excessive iron in the diet. If your bird's diet has excessive Vitamin C, iron is absorbed faster into the body. Even an excessive intake of Vitamin A leads to iron storage diseases.

It is best that you avoid nectars fortified with iron, juices, baby foods and other products that contain a lot of iron. Some table scraps can also be harmful to birds as they contain ferrous sulfate which is even more harmful for your Umbrella Cockatoos.

Lung and Respiratory disorders

Respiratory and lung disorders in birds are normally caused by fungi, bacteria or parasites. With most of these conditions, treatment is only effective when provided at an early stage of the disease.

Aspergillosis

This is, perhaps, the most common respiratory condition in cockatoos. There are two forms of this disease. The first type occurs in young birds or birds that have been imported due to the exposure to spores of a fungus called *Aspergillosis*. There is another form of this condition that is more severe. It occurs in birds that live in poorly ventilated areas. Here, the pores are concentrated in these areas and are inhaled into the air sacs of the birds.

Any stress triggers the condition and the bird will begin to show severe symptoms. Vitamin A deficiency is also a trigger for this condition as it weakens the respiratory system of the bird. Immunity is compromised and the bird develops the chronic form of this condition.

The lower respiratory tract is usually affected by this disease. The trachea, bronchii and the voice organ are also affected along with the air sacs. It is also possible that the infection spreads to other organs from the respiratory tract.

There are a few signs of infection that you will have to watch out for. This includes sudden loss of appetite, strained breathing and inflammation of the air sacs. Death occurs suddenly in most cases because this disease spreads so rapidly.

When the bird is affected by a chronic form of aspergillosis, you will notice fatigue, depression, changes in the voice, labored breathing and even emaciation. The architecture of the respiratory system may also get damaged when the infection becomes too severe.

The only preventive measure against this condition is good hygiene along with a well-balanced diet. You also need to make sure that the cage is well ventilated to avoid any concentration of the fungal spores that are mostly responsible for this condition.

Avian influenza

This is a condition that is usually spread from wild birds to domestic birds. This disease has become a big concern among bird owners simply because it also has the potential to harm human beings in the long run. Several mutations have been observed in this condition, making it more dangerous for human beings.

The Centre for Disease Control and Prevention in the USA has altogether banned any import of birds from certain countries in Asia, Europe and Africa where the disease is prevalent.

This virus is transmitted from one bird to another when they come in contact with each other's feces or respiratory secretion. The most common signs of disease include loss of appetite, swelling of the head, diarrhea, discharge from the eyes and strained breathing. In some cases, the birds may just recover on their own and in other cases, they may die before you are able to notice any symptoms.

Any sign of respiratory diseases requires immediate attention from an Avian vet. You will also have to isolate the bird to ensure that the disease does not spread with the flock.

The disease is usually treated by antibiotics. Vaccines are available to prevent the condition as well. The best way to keep your pet safe is to ensure that there is no contact between your bird and wild birds. Even when you use a piece of wood from the outdoors as a perch for your bird, make sure that it is cleaned perfectly. Any chance of coming in contact with wild birds' environment should be prevented.

Kidney related disorders
One of the most common kidney related conditions in birds is gout. In this condition, an abnormal amount of uric acid crystals accumulate in the body. The liver is responsible for the production of these crystals while the kidney helps excrete them. However, when the kidney fails to remove these crystals effectively from the bloodstream of the bird, the crystals develop all over the body.

This condition normally occurs when you do not give your bird a balanced meal. If the protein levels are higher than recommended, gout may occur. Too much calcium or very little vitamin A can also cause this condition in birds. Usually, the joint is very badly affected and can be extremely painful.

In conditions where the pain is beyond control with medication, vets opt for euthanasia. The crystals can be removed surgically if they are not very close to the blood vessels. If the proximity is too close, there are chances that severe bleeding may occur during the surgery, killing the bird.

Oral medicines can be prescribed in the initial stages of the condition. If not treated immediately, gout may even affect the internal organs of the bird. The membranes of most of the vital organs are covered by these crystals, leading to death eventually.

Besides the diet, genetics and the environment also play a very important role in the development of gout in birds. This is one of the reasons why regular veterinary examination is a must. If gout is detected early, your bird can be cured with simple medicines and good care.

Multi organ diseases
There are several infections that can destroy various parts of your bird's body rapidly when it manifests. These are usually bacterial or viral infections that are quite hard to treat effectively.

Polyomavirus
This is a type of virus that will affect a bird of any age. However, juveniles and hatchlings are most susceptible to this condition. Birds will show a depletion in appetite, sudden weakness, diarrhea and even bruising in the skin or the muscles. This infection usually targets the kidneys, the liver and the heart of the bird. There is very little chance for a bird to survive this infection as it spreads rapidly, leading to death in just 24 to 48 hours.

In a rare case when the bird does survive, there is severe lung and heart damage as well as abnormal feather growth. These birds then become carriers of the condition and may spread the condition among the flock.

This virus is spread from the female birds to the egg. But, mostly the infection occurs when a bird comes in contact with the feather dander of an affected bird. There is no treatment available for this condition. The best thing you can do when you detect the symptoms in one of your birds is to isolate it.

Vaccinations are available for hatchlings. You can provide two doses of this vaccine; the first one when the bird is about 4 weeks old and the second one after 2 more weeks. Booster shots are given annually to prevent the condition.

You can also take preventive measures by keeping the cage clean. You need to disinfect the feeders, incubators and even nesting boxes regularly. A vet can help you with the standard procedures of hygiene that can effectively control the manifestation of this disease in birds.

Pacheco's disease

This is a condition that spreads very rapidly in all species of parrots. It is caused by a certain strain of herpes virus. Any stress can lead to a manifestation of symptoms. Birds become more susceptible to this condition under stress, too. It is spread when a bird comes in contact with an affected bird directly. It is also airborne or waterborne. It is common for old world parrots to be carriers of this condition.

The signs of this condition are noticed just days before the bird is about to die. The birds are in great shape with a healthy appetite until then. Suddenly, you will notice fluffing, watery feces and loss of energy in the birds. Very few birds recover from an infection like this.

There are several other herpes virus related conditions like papillomas that may either be internal or external. In Umbrella Cockatoos, internal papillomas are normally noticed. It is believed that these internal papillomas are caused by a virus that is closely related to the Pacheco's disease herpes virus. Another uncommon infection in Umbrella Cockatoos is Amazon tracheitis, which is the inflammation of the trachea. This is another condition related to herpes virus.

Psittacossis

Also known as chlamydiosis, this condition is caused by a bacterial called *Chlamydophiliaa psittaci*. This bacteria is commonly seen in the stool of the infected bird or the nasal secretions of the birds. Since this disease is easily transmitted from birds to people, you need to follow several regulatory practices with respect to quarantining a bird when you bring it home or when it is suspected of having the condition. In many parts of the world, a ban on direct imports of these birds from South America has actually reduced the prevalence of the condition.

In some birds, there is a genetic predisposition to not become ill when they are infected. Such birds will remain carriers of the condition though.

The signs of psittacosis usually include depression, ruffled feathers, reduced vocalization or appetite and discharge from the nose and the eyes. In some cases, lime green droppings are also noticed.

There is another form of psittacosis that affects the central nervous system of the bird. In this case, the bird will show signs like twisting of the head, shaking, tremors and even convulsions. While this condition is predominant in old world parrots, you need to make sure that you take enough preventive measures for your Umbrella Cockatoo as well.

When this condition has been diagnosed, antibiotics are given to the bird through the food or water. Birds that have this condition will require a lot of supportive care. They need to be isolated, given the adequate amount of heat, absence of stress and of course lots of fluids and good quality food.

Keeping the bird away from potential sources of infection is the best way to prevent the disease. This bacteria will lie dormant for many years and may suddenly manifest in case of stress. These bacteria are usually found in dry feces. Therefore, regular care and cleaning of the cage is very important. There is always a chance of reinfection if necessary steps are not taken to maintain hygiene.

Remember to protect yourself while handling a sick bird as you are also susceptible to this condition. Make sure that you wear gloves. After you handle the contents of the cage or the bird, make sure that you thoroughly wash and disinfect your hands. It is necessary, in some states, to report this condition to the local health authorities to coordinate the treatment procedures with the respective government agency.

Reproductive disorders
There are always chances of complications and issues when your bird is in the breeding season. Reproductive diseases could be recurring or may be prevalent for a few breeding seasons. Some of the most common reproductive diseases in cockatoos include:

Cloacal prolapse or vent prolapse

The cloaca is that part of the bird where the feces and urine is passed from. The outermost part of this region is called the vent. This vent will control the frequency of droppings in birds. When the inner tissue begins to protrude through the vent, the condition is known as cloacal prolapse or vent prolapse. It is caused by several physiological and psychological conditions that affect the bird. It is necessary to have your bird checked by a veterinarian immediately after you notice the prolapse.

The exact cause for this condition still remains unexplained. It is noticed, however, that it is more common in birds that have been hand raised or have been weaned wrongly. Some birds also have the tendency to hold in their stool, leading to a prolapse.

Surgery and behavior modification are the best remedies to this issue. The hardest part, of course, is modifying the behavior of the bird. In many cases, the close bond between the owner and the bird breaks after the onset of this condition. Sometimes, the bond needs to be broken when the bird has a misplaced sexual emotion towards the owner. Yes, many times the birds believe that their owner is the mate. This leads to a lot of stress, causing prolapse.

In order to break this bond, the owners must restrict hand feeding, stroking the bird on the back or even holding the bird close to his or her body. In case you are unable to change the behavior of the bird, you can look for an animal behavior consultant as well.

Egg binding

Sometimes, the female bird is unable to lay the egg properly. It is difficult for her to expel the egg. This condition is very common in birds that are overweight. If your bird is not properly stimulated physically and mentally, this condition may occur.

Another common causal factor for this condition is calcium deficiency. Medium to large sized birds are very prone to egg binding. Therefore, you need to take extra care of your Umbrella Cockatoos during the breeding season.

There are a few signs of egg binding, including swaying while walking, unsteady posture, inability to stay up on the perch, wagging of the tail, abdominal swelling etc. Paralysis is also possible if the egg puts any pressure on the nerves of the bird. You must never attempt to remove the egg yourself as you may end up paralyzing or killing the bird.

When you notice these signs, take the bird to a vet. An X-ray is taken to determine the extent of the condition and to locate the egg in the bird's reproductive tract. There are several methods like hydration, lubrication, additional warmth and calcium supplementation that are used to remove the egg. Abnormalities in the egg will also be tested.

You can provide the bird with various injections like prostaglandins and oxytocin. This will help move the egg along and finally out of the bird. However, when these methods fail, the only option is to remove the egg surgically. Some vets will also try to manually remove the egg if there is no risk of damage caused to the bird's health.

When you notice even a slight deviation from the normal in your bird, consult your vet immediately. This is the key to ensure that your bird is healthier for longer.

4. Injuries and accidents

There are several accidents and injuries that birds are susceptible to. They may get into fights with one another, fly into windows or even suffer from poisoning. Now, these are emergencies that you have to deal with immediately. But first, you need to identify what is causing distress to your birds in the first place. Here are some common accidents with respect to birds:

Heavy metal poisoning

Metals like zinc and lead are common in our environment. That is why you need to take extra care to ensure that your birds do not get exposed to them for long. It is best that you never let your bird get outside the cage without any supervision. You must also carefully inspect the bird's environment and make sure that there are no sources of these heavy metals like fencing and even the cage material around the bird. Selecting the cage material carefully is one of the best preventive measures against metal poisoning.

Zinc poisoning is more common than lead poisoning because of the process of galvanization that has become so popular today. This is used in construction of wiring material and even the cage itself. As for lead, the common sources are lead weights used in fishing, curtain weights, stained glass, old paint etc.

Excessive thirst, depression, weakness and regurgitation of water are the most common signs of heavy metal poisoning in birds. In some cases, lack of coordination, excessive trembling and even seizures are observed.

An X-ray of the bird is taken to determine the presence of any metals in the gizzard of the bird. Blood tests are also required to check for any metal in the blood stream. Medication called chelating agents are given to the bird along with supportive care when poisoning is detected. This is usually injected into the bird's muscle. When the bird is stable, you can even administer this agent orally to the bird. The response to treatment is usually quite rapid, provided that it is not too severe.

Fume or aerosol poisoning
Overheating surfaces that contain Teflon, Tefzel and Silverstone can release fumes that are toxic for birds. Most nonstick cookware, self-cleaning ovens and irons have a coating of fluropolymers. This material will begin to release particles when heated slightly. The particles that are released are toxic for the birds.

Besides this , there are various other chemical hazards in our homes that can affect the birds. Aerosol products including deodorants, carpet fresheners, room fresheners, oven cleaners and other substances like plastic can be sources of irritants and toxins for birds. Smoke is one of the most dangerous things for the birds in your home.

The common signs of fume or aerosol poisoning include neurological symptoms like tremors, labored breathing and even sudden death. Normally, even the slightest exposure is deadly for the bird, giving the owner no time to get the bird away from the environment. It is best to be cautious and make sure that your bird's cage is placed in such a way that it is not close to any sources of these toxic fumes. The cage should also be in a room that is very well ventilated to prevent any accumulation of these toxins.

Fractures

Broken bones and dislocations are quite common among pet birds. The problem with the bones in birds is that they are filled with air and are actually part of the respiratory system of the bird. In addition to that, the bones are also quite brittle leading to multiple fractures when the bird has an accident.

If you notice that your bird has a dislocated wing or broken wing, it is best not to touch the bird. Contact your vet immediately to prevent any further damage. He will be able to guide you through the process of stabilizing the bone of your beloved pet. Rigid stabilization is good enough in most cases, as bird bones heal rather quickly. Only in extreme conditions will surgery be required to restore the normal function of the bones that are affected.

Physical therapy is also recommended for birds with broken bones. This is to ensure that the joints do not become frozen and stiff, reducing the range of motion of the area. An orthopedic specialist is usually recommended to help your bird recover faster.

Preparing a first aid kit

A first aid kit is a must in a home with any pets. In the case of birds, too, you need to prepare a first aid kit that can help you provide emergency care to the bird when required. The items you need to include are:

- The number and directions to your veterinary clinic or the emergency facility suggested by your avian vet.
- Phone numbers for poison control. You will be able to get this information from your vet.
- Scissors in order to remove any strings or to cut bandaging material.
- Sterilized gauze
- Q-tips to clean up a wound and to apply any topical medicine.
- Tape
- A roll of clean gauze to wrap a wing that is injured.
- Antibiotic cream recommended by the vet.
- Styptic pencil to control bleeding.
- Betadine or Hydrogen peroxide to clean any wound.
- Pliers or tweezers to handle small bandages and tapes.

- Heating pad to help a bird experiencing chilling.
- An ink dropper to administer internal medication.
- Large towels to handle the bird.
- Thermometer to measure the temperature of the bird's body.

Keep all of the above in a box that is easily accessible and make sure that your family is aware of the different situations that may require the first aid kit. They also need to be told how the bird can be helped in case of common accidents and injuries around the house.

5. Preventive Measures

Prevention is always better than cure. It is really heartbreaking to see your beloved pet wallow in pain and die an unexpected death. Instead of multiple veterinary meetings, it is a good idea to take a few simple preventive measures to keep your birds safe:

- **Keep them away from wild birds or animals:** The cage should be kept in an area that is not accessible to any wild birds or rodents like mice that generally carry a lot of disease causing microbes. The food and water should not be contaminated by them. Any spilled food or litter should be cleaned up immediately to make sure that these creatures are not attracted.

- **Clean up as much as you can:** The housing area of the bird must be pristine. The most common breeding grounds for bacteria, parasites and viruses include organic matter in the cage such as the feces.

    Make sure that the cage is cleaned on a regular basis. You need to be additionally cautious if you are planning to keep the birds outdoors.
    You must make it a rule not to borrow equipment or allow other bird owners to handle your Umbrella Cockatoo. This can lead to the transmission of unwanted feather dander or microbe carrying debris.

- **Keep an eye on your bird:** Be an attentive bird parent. If your Umbrella Cockatoo shows the slightest deviation from what you consider normal, become alert. You may have to take your bird to the vet to have him examined completely. It may seem like

104

you are too overprotective at times. However, it is necessary that you catch any disease as early as you can to provide suitable treatment to help the bird cope with it and recover fast.

- **Follow good quarantining:** Make sure that any new bird that is included in the flock is quarantined properly. Most often, a bird could simply be a carrier of the condition. When kept in quarantine, you will be able to observe the bird for any abnormalities. This can be treated effectively before it spreads to other birds in your household. Even if you plan to take your bird to shows or exhibitions, you will have to quarantine him for at least two weeks before reintroducing him to the flock. A great way to ensure that your bird is not a carrier is to find a good breeder who practices strict disease control at his center.

- **Regular vet visits:** Your bird needs to be checked regularly for any chance of infections. Make sure that you never miss your annual veterinary checkup if you want to keep your bird in good health at all times. Here are a few recommended tests that you should have the vet conduct to be sure that your bird is free from deadly diseases.

Adult birds:
- Complete blood count to make sure that there are no internal infections.
- Study of culture to diagnose any possibility of yeast or bacterial infection.
- Full body X-ray.

Young birds:
- Complete Blood Count to check for any internal infections.
- Chlamydophilia Immunoassay in order to diagnose parrot fever that is highly contagious, affecting birds and human beings.
- Culture study to eliminate chances of yeast or bacterial infections.

You can never be too sure of the right methods to take good care of your bird. However, you can be a good parent by eliminating all the chances of the disease and reduce the risk for your beloved Umbrella

Cockatoo. With these preventive measures you can take care of most deadly conditions easily.

6. Insurance for your bird

Treating a sick bird can be really expensive. With each visit that you pay to your vet, you may spend anything between $50-100 / £25-50. If your bird is diagnosed with a health condition, especially, this can become a recurring expense that is quite hard to deal with.

Unfortunately, it is not common to find insurance companies willing to insure pet birds. The primary reason for this is that they are prone to health issues that can escalate very quickly. The best option for most bird owners is to set aside a fixed amount each month for healthcare from the time you purchase your bird.

There are some brands of insurance providers that do have some options available for birds. They are:

- Pet Assure
- ExoticDirect
- Leisure Guard Insurance
- You also have the option of VPI which is short for Veterinary Pet Insurance. This insurance does allow you to see any preferred veterinarian. However, they do put a limit on the number of visits and the cover that they offer annually. So, you may not be able to get full coverage for any major procedure that your bird may have to undergo.

No matter what insurance plan you choose, make sure that they cover the following:
- Veterinary charges: They will pay for certain diagnostic procedures like X-rays and even some consultation fees. Veterinarian costs will mostly include emergencies only. In the case of birds like the Umbrella Cockatoo that have long lives, there may be a limit on the cover offered annually that may go up to $1500 or £3000.

- Escape or Loss/ Death: If you lose your bird to theft or death, they may cover some amount of the market value of an exotic bird. Theft and Escape cover requires you to fulfill some security conditions such as purchasing a five lever lock for the cage door.

- Public Liability: This covers any damage caused by your bird to another person or property.

- Overseas cover: This is necessary for you to travel with your pet to some countries.

The cost of your insurance with all these covers will come up to about $150 or £280 a month. These covers are purchased separately and you can cut costs on things like overseas cover or public liability cover if you do not think that it is necessary. However, all these covers are highly recommended for all pet owners. You can compare the costs of various insurance plans online to find one that works for you. If you have multiple birds, some of them may also offer a 10% discount on the insurance cover.

The cover that you will get for your bird depends upon the species, the age of the bird and whether or not it is an exotic species. If you do not have any insurance policy for birds in your country, it is best to save money for medical expenses in a separate account.

Chapter 7: Cost of Owning an Umbrella Cockatoo

Umbrella Cockatoos are a big financial responsibility. Therefore, you need to be sure that you can sustain the costs involved. You should have enough funds available to take care of the bird for a good 30 years at least. Here is a break-down of the cost of owning an Umbrella Cockatoo.

The minimum expenses include:

•   Cost of the bird: If you decide to adopt an Umbrella Cockatoo, it will cost you approximately $150 or £75. If you buy a bird from a breeder or a pet store, it will cost you about $650-100 or £350-800.

•   Cost of the cage: You must never compromise on the quality of the cage and ensure that your bird gets nothing but the best. A good cage will cost you about $180-400 or £100-200. It should be made from good material and should be secure for the bird.

•   Food Expenses: It is necessary to give your parrot a good mixture of fresh produce and pellets. Of course, you need to add treats as well. If you add up all the costs, it will come up to at least $50 or £30 each month.

•   Veterinary costs: Veterinary costs will go up to $1200 or £800 annually. On average, every consultation should cost you close to $50 or £30.

•   Toys: You need to keep buying new toys to keep an Umbrella Cockatoo entertained. You can expect to spend at least $30 or £15 each month on the toys alone.

•   Insurance: As discussed before, insurance can cost up to $250 or £150 each month, depending upon the coverage that you opt for.

On average you could spend close to $400 or £200 each month on bird care. Before you bring a bird home, make sure that you take this sum out of your monthly income and put it away. If you are able to manage all your expenses for the month and if you can keep this up for at least three months, you are ready for the financial commitment of an Umbrella Cockatoo. If not, you may have to wait a little longer or figure out how you will manage these expenses.

Conclusion

If you are reading this book, it means that you are already on your way to becoming a responsible pet parent. This book is designed to help beginners and also those with some experience with parrots or other types of birds learn about the specific needs of the Umbrella Cockatoo.

The idea is to ensure that all pet owners are able to provide the right care from the first day of the bird in their homes. If your queries and doubts about whether you should bring home an Umbrella Cockatoo or not are answered, then the book has served its purpose.

If you have decided to bring home your beloved pet, then you are in for a wonderful journey. Make sure that you are constantly upgrading your knowledge about these birds to provide your pet with the best possible care.

If the book showed you that you are not ready for a pet of your own, then you can start out by fostering birds and learning more about them. And, when you are ready, you will have all the help that you need with this book and you can prepare for your new companion.

References

As mentioned before, there is no end to learning about Umbrella Cockatoos. One of the best sources for news and discussions is the Internet. Here are some reliable sources that you can choose to learn more about these birds:

- www.whitecockatoo.com
- www.iaate.org
- www.cockatoo-info.com
- www.goldencockatoo.wordpress.com
- www.goodbirdinc.com
- www.parrotblog.org
- www.certapet.com
- www.parrotmag.com
- www.littlepeckers.co.uk
- www.australiangeographic.com.au
- www.birdsupplies.com
- www.what-when-how.com
- www.upatsix.com
- www.animals.nationalgeographic.com
- www.parrotsdailynews.com
- www.birdchannel.com
- www.beautyofbirds.com
  www.premiumparrots.com
- www.lafeber.com
- www.bagheera.com
- www.thegabrielfoundation.org
- www.peteducation.com
- www.animal-world.com
- www.petparrot.com
- www.parrotsecrets.com
- www.birdtricks.com
- www.au.answers.yahoo.com
- www.neotropical.birds.cornell.edu
- www.rioyou.blogspot.in
- www.parrotislandinc.com
- www.parrotsinternational.org

CPSIA information can be obtained
at www.ICGtesting.com
Printed in the USA
LVHW082233120421
684319LV00034B/992